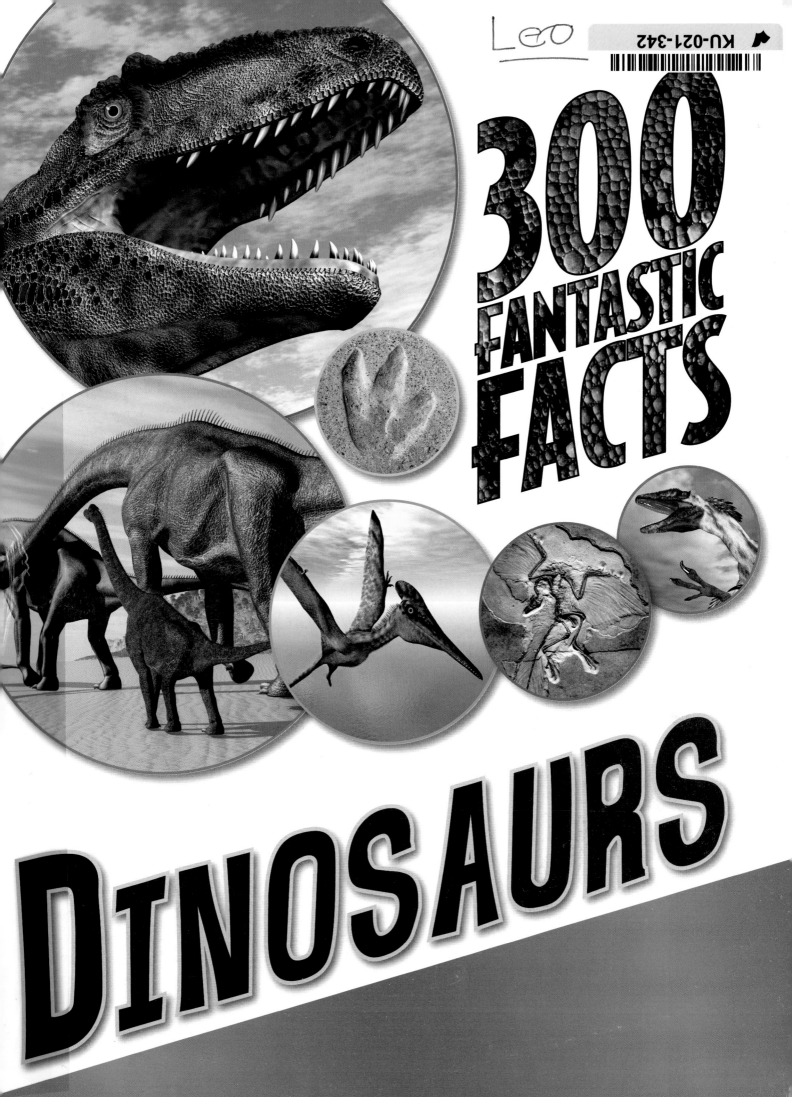

300 FANTASTIC FACTS

DINOSAURS

300 FANTASTIC FACTS

DINOSAURS

Written by: Rupert Matthews, Steve Parker

Miles Kelly

First published in 2015 by Miles Kelly Publishing Ltd
Harding's Barn, Bardfield End Green, Thaxted, Essex, CM6 3PX, UK

Copyright © Miles Kelly Publishing Ltd 2015

2 4 6 8 10 9 7 5 3 1

Publishing Director Belinda Gallagher
Creative Director Jo Cowan
Designers Rob Hale, Andrea Slane
Cover Designer Rob Hale
Editorial Assistant Meghan Oosterhuis
Image Manager Liberty Newton
Production Manager Elizabeth Collins
Reprographics Stephan Davis, Jennifer Cozens, Thom Allaway
Consultant Steve Parker
Indexer Jane Parker

ISBN 978-1-78209-738-9

Printed in China

British Library Cataloguing-in-Publication Data
A catalogue record for this book is available from the British Library

Made with paper from a sustainable forest

www.mileskelly.net
info@mileskelly.net

Contents

PREHISTORIC LIFE

1 **The Earth was once covered by huge sheets of ice.** This happened several times during Earth's history and we call these frozen times ice ages. However, the ice ages are a tiny part of prehistory. Before then, the world was warm and lakes and seas covered the land. Even earlier than this, there was little rain for thousands of years, and the land was covered in deserts. Over millions of years weather and conditions changed. Living things changed too, in order to survive. This change is called 'evolution'.

Woolly rhinoceros

Cave lion

▼ A scene from the last ice age, about 10,000 years ago. Animals grew thick fur coats to protect themselves from the cold. Many animals, such as woolly mammoths, survived on plants such as mosses. Others, such as cave lions, were fierce hunters, needing meat to survive.

Aurochs

Woolly mammoth

Megaloceros

Life begins

2 Life began a very, very long time ago. We know this from the remains of prehistoric life forms that died and were buried. Over millions of years, their remains turned into shapes in rocks, called fossils. The first fossils are over 3000 million years old. They are tiny 'blobs' called bacteria – living things that still survive today.

3 The first plants were seaweeds, which appeared about 1000 million years ago. Unlike bacteria and blue-green algae, which each had just one living cell, these plants had thousands of cells. Some seaweeds were many metres long. They were called algae – the same name that scientists use today.

4 By about 800 million years ago, some plants were starting to grow on land. They were mixed with other living things called moulds, or fungi. Together, the algae (plants) and fungi formed flat green-and-yellow crusts that crept over rocks and soaked up rain. They were called lichens. These still grow on rocks and trees today.

▼ Fossils of *Anomalocaris* have been found in Canada. It had a circular mouth and fin-like body parts. Its body was covered by a shell.

Jellyfish

5 **The first animals lived in the sea – and they were as soft as jelly!** Over 600 million years ago, some of the first animals were jellyfish, floating in the water. On the seabed lived groups of soft, feathery-looking creatures called *Charnia*. This animal was an early type of coral. Animals need to take in food by eating other living things. *Charnia* caught tiny plants in its 'feathers'.

◀ *Charnia* looked like a prehistoric plant, but it was actually an animal!

Charnia

6 **One of the first hunting animals was *Anomalocaris*.** It lived 520 million years ago, swimming through the sea in search of prey. It caught smaller creatures in its pincers, then pushed them into its mouth. *Anomalocaris* was a cousin of crabs and insects. It was one of the biggest hunting animals of its time, even though it was only 60 centimetres long.

7 **By 400 million years ago, plants on land were growing taller.** They had stiff stems that held them upright and carried water to their topmost parts. An early upright plant was *Cooksonia*. It was the tallest living thing on land, at just 5 centimetres tall – hardly the size of your thumb!

▲ The *Cooksonia* plant had forked stems that carried water. The earliest examples have been found in Ireland.

Animals swarm the seas

8 **Some of the first common animals were worms.** However, they were not earthworms in soil. At the time there was no soil and the land was bare. These worms lived in the sea. They burrowed in mud for plants and animals to eat.

◀ *Ottoia* was a sea worm that fed by filtering tiny food particles from the sea.

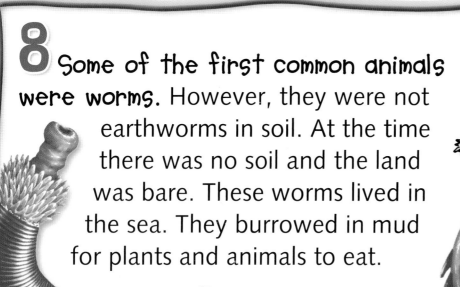

▼ Trilobites moved quickly across the seabed. Some could roll up into a ball like woodlice do today. This was a means of protection.

9 **The next animals to become common were trilobites.** They first lived about 550 million years ago in the sea. Trilobites crawled along the seabed eating tiny bits of food they found. Their name means 'three lobes' (parts). A trilobite had two grooves along its back, from head to tail, so its body had three main parts – left, middle and centre.

▼ *Pterygotus* was a fierce hunter, with large eyes and long claws.

10 **Trilobites were some of the first animals with legs that bent at the joints.** Animals with jointed legs are called arthropods. They have been the most common creatures for millions of years, including trilobites long ago, and later on, crabs, spiders and insects. Like other arthropods, trilobites had a tough, outer shell for protection.

11 **Some of the first hunters were sea scorpions — some were as big as lions!** *Pterygotus* was 2 metres long. It swished its tail to chase prey through water, which it tore apart with its huge claws. Sea scorpions lived 500– 250 million years ago. Unlike modern scorpions, they had no sting in their tails.

12 For millions of years the seabed was covered with the curly shells of ammonites. Some of these shells were as small as your fingernail, others were bigger than dinner plates. Ammonites were successful creatures and thousands of kinds survived for millions of years. Each ammonite had big eyes to see prey and long tentacles (arms) to catch it with. Ammonites died out at the same time as the dinosaurs, around 65 million years ago.

▲ This rock contains an ammonite fossil. The shell would have protected the soft-bodied creature inside.

◄ *Pikaia* looked a little bit like an eel with fins.

13 Among the worms, trilobites and ammonites was a small creature that had a very special body part – the beginnings of a backbone. It was called *Pikaia* and lived about 530 million years ago. Gradually, more animals with backbones, called vertebrates, evolved from it. Today, vertebrates rule much of the world – they are fish, reptiles, birds and mammals.

QUIZ

1. Did sea scorpions have stings in their tails?
2. What does the name 'trilobite' mean?
3. What kind of animal was *Ottoia*?
4. When did ammonites die out?
5. What was special about *Pikaia*?

Answers:
1. No 2. Three lobes, or parts 3. A worm 4. 65 million years ago 5. It had an early type of backbone

Very fishy

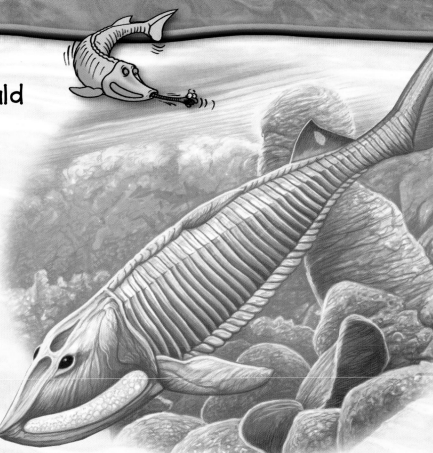

14 The first fish could not bite – they were suckers! About 500 million years ago, new animals appeared in the sea – the first fish. They had no jaws or teeth and probably sucked in worms and small pieces of food from the mud.

15 Some early fish wore suits of armour! They had hard, curved plates of bone all over their bodies for protection. These fish were called placoderms and most were fierce hunters. Some had huge jaws with sharp sheets of bone for slicing up prey.

▲ *Hemicyclaspis* was an early jawless fish. It had eyes on top of its head and probably lived on the seabed. This way it could keep a look out for predators above.

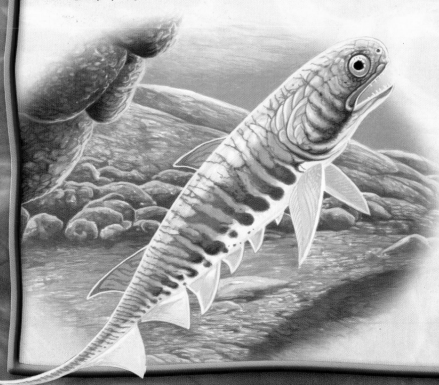

16 Spiny sharks had spines, but they were not really sharks. These fish were similar in shape to today's sharks, but they lived in rivers and lakes, not the sea, about 430 million years ago. *Climatius* was a spiny shark that looked fierce, but it was only as big as your finger!

◄ The fins on the back of *Climatius* were supported by needle-sharp spines. These helped to protect it from attacks by squid or other fish.

17

The first really big hunting fish was bigger than today's great white shark! *Dunkleosteus* grew to almost 10 metres in length and swam in the oceans 360 million years ago. It sliced up prey, such as other fish, using its massive teeth made of narrow blades of bone, each one as big as this book.

18

Some early fish started to 'walk' out of water. Types of fish called lobefins appeared 390 million years ago. Their side fins each had a 'stump' at the base made of muscle. If the water in their pool dried up, lobefins could use their fins like stubby legs to waddle over land to another pool. *Eusthenopteron* was a lobefin fish about one metre long. Over millions of years, some lobefins evolved into four-legged animals called tetrapods.

VERY FISHY!

You will need:
waxed card (like the kind used to make milk cartons) crayons scissors piece of soap

Place the piece of waxed card face down. Fold the card up at the edges. Draw a fish on the card. Cut a small notch in the rear of the card and wedge the piece of soap in it. Put the 'fish' in a bath of cold water and watch it swim away.

▼ *Eusthenopteron* could clamber about on dry land when moving from one stretch of water to another.

Animals invade the land

19 The first land animals lived about 450 million years ago. These early creatures, which came from the sea, were arthropods – creatures with hard outer body casings and jointed legs. They included prehistoric insects, spiders and millipedes. *Arthropleura* was a millipede – it was 2 metres in length!

▶ *Arthropleura* was as long as a human and was the largest-ever land arthropod.

20 Some amphibians were fierce hunters. *Gerrothorax* was about one metre long and spent most of its time at the bottom of ponds or streams. Its eyes pointed upward, to see fish swimming past, just above. *Gerrothorax* would then jump up to grab the fish in its wide jaws.

21 The first four-legged animal had eight toes on each front foot! *Acanthostega* used its toes to grip water plants as it swam. It lived about 380 million years ago and was one metre long. Creatures like it soon began to walk on land, too. They were called tetrapods, which means 'four legs'. They were a big advance in evolution – the first land animals with backbones.

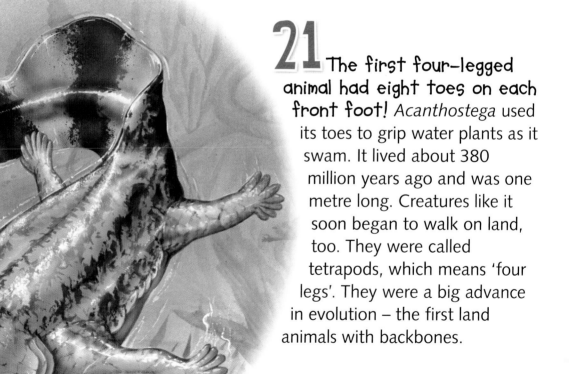

◀ *Acanthostega* probably spent most of its time in water. It had gills for breathing underwater as well as lungs for breathing air.

22 Soon four-legged animals called amphibians were racing across the land. Amphibians were the first backboned animals to move fast out of the water. *Aphaneramma* had long legs and could run quickly. However, prehistoric amphibians, like those of today such as frogs and newts, had to return to the water to lay their eggs.

23 Fins became legs for walking on land, and tails changed, too. As the fins of lobefin fish evolved into legs, their tails became longer and more muscular. *Ichthyostega* had a long tail with a fin along its upper side. This tail design was good for swimming in water, and also helpful when wriggling across a swamp.

24 Some amphibians grew as big as crocodiles! *Eogyrinus* was almost 5 metres long and had strong jaws and teeth, like a crocodile. However, it lived about 300 million years ago, long before any crocodiles appeared. Although *Eogyrinus* could walk on dry land, it spent most of its time in streams and swamps.

◄ *Ichthyostega* had short legs, so it could probably only move slowly on land.

Life after death

25 There were times in prehistory when almost everything died out. These times are called mass extinctions. Just a few types of plants and animals survive, which can then change, or evolve, into new kinds. A mass extinction about 290 million years ago allowed a fairly new group of animals to spread fast – the reptiles.

26 Reptiles' skin and eggs helped them to survive. Unlike an amphibian's, a reptile's scaly skin was waterproof. Also, the jelly-like eggs of amphibians had to be laid in water, while a reptile's eggs had tough shells for surviving on land. Around 280 million years ago, reptiles such as 1.5-metre-long *Varanosaurus* were spreading to dry areas where amphibians could not survive.

EDIBLE REPTILES!

You will need:
100 grams dried milk 100 grams smooth peanut butter 2 tablespoons honey currants food colouring

Mix the dried milk, peanut butter and honey in a bowl. Mould this paste into reptile shapes. Decorate with currants for eyes and add food colouring for bright skin patterns. Then cause a mass extinction – eat them!

▲ *Varanosaurus* lived in what is now Texas, USA, and may have hunted fish in swamps.

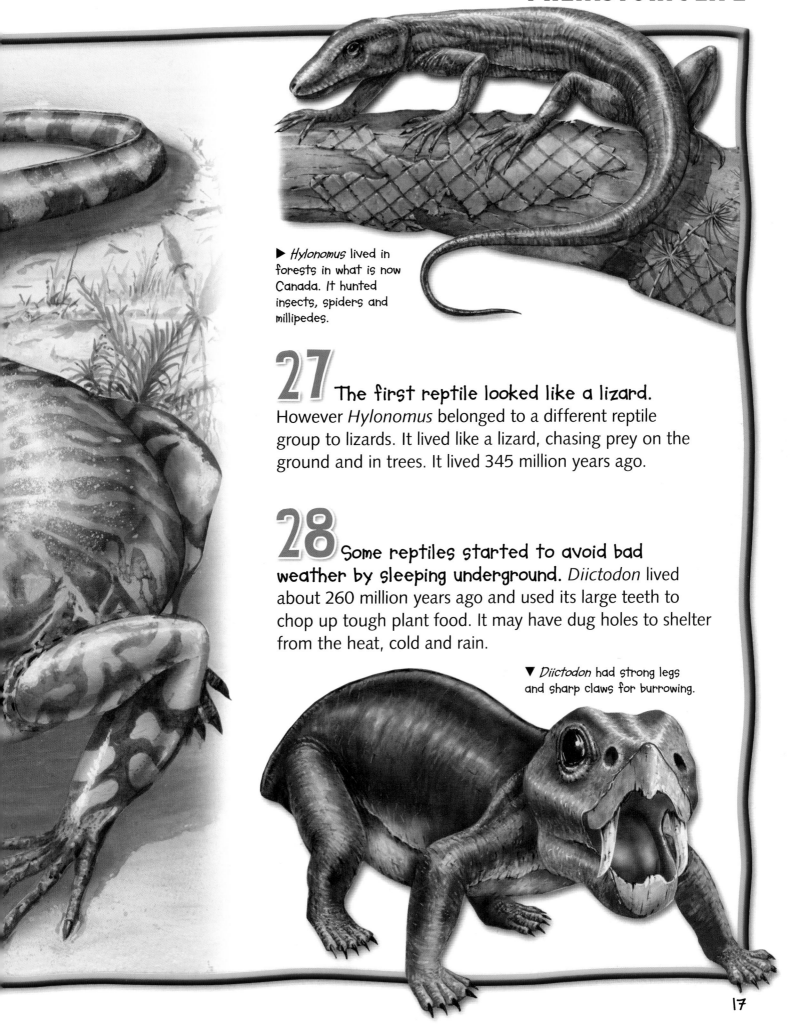

▶ *Hylonomus* lived in forests in what is now Canada. It hunted insects, spiders and millipedes.

27 **The first reptile looked like a lizard.** However *Hylonomus* belonged to a different reptile group to lizards. It lived like a lizard, chasing prey on the ground and in trees. It lived 345 million years ago.

28 **Some reptiles started to avoid bad weather by sleeping underground.** *Diictodon* lived about 260 million years ago and used its large teeth to chop up tough plant food. It may have dug holes to shelter from the heat, cold and rain.

▼ *Diictodon* had strong legs and sharp claws for burrowing.

Wars around the world

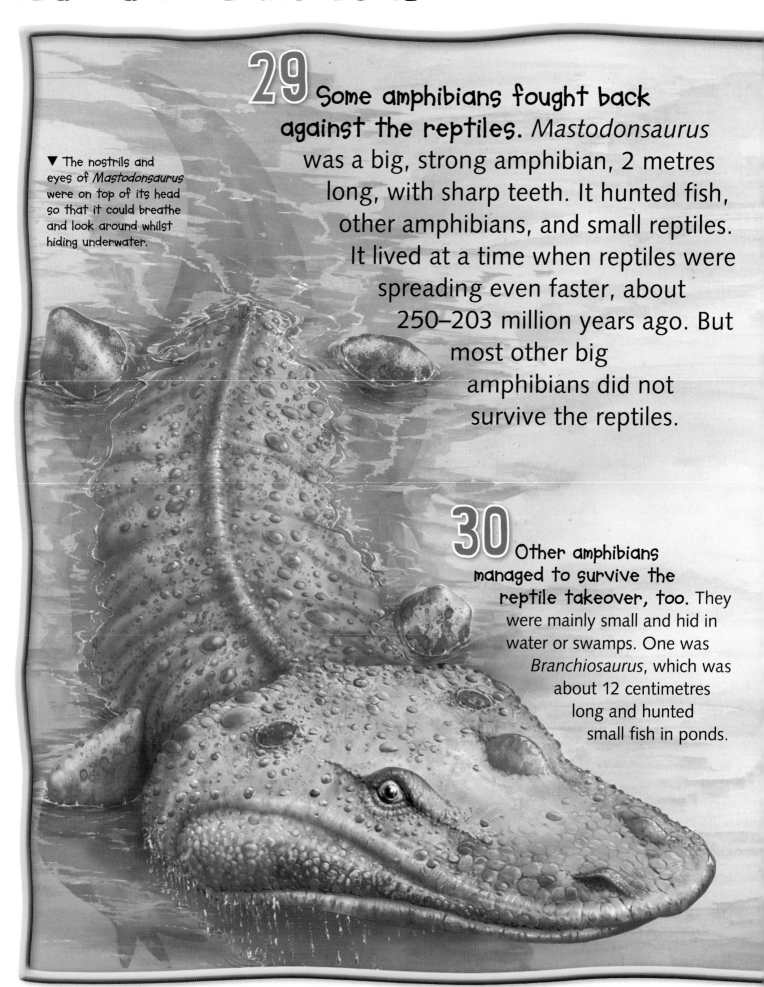

▼ The nostrils and eyes of *Mastodonsaurus* were on top of its head so that it could breathe and look around whilst hiding underwater.

29 Some amphibians fought back against the reptiles. *Mastodonsaurus* was a big, strong amphibian, 2 metres long, with sharp teeth. It hunted fish, other amphibians, and small reptiles. It lived at a time when reptiles were spreading even faster, about 250–203 million years ago. But most other big amphibians did not survive the reptiles.

30 Other amphibians managed to survive the reptile takeover, too. They were mainly small and hid in water or swamps. One was *Branchiosaurus*, which was about 12 centimetres long and hunted small fish in ponds.

31 *Mastodonsaurus* may have had tusks sticking out of its nose! Two front teeth may have poked through holes at the end of its snout.

▲ *Lystrosaurus* lived in Antarctica when it was a land of lush, tropical plant life. Today it is a frozen continent, covered by thick ice.

32 Reptiles showed how the world's lands moved about. *Lystrosaurus* lived about 200 million years ago and its fossils come from Europe, Asia, Africa and Antarctica. This reptile could not swim, so all of these landmasses, or continents, must have been joined together at one time. Over millions of years, they drifted apart to form today's positions.

33 Some plant-eating reptiles had very sharp teeth. *Moschops* was as big as a rhino and lived in southern Africa about 270 million years ago. Its teeth were long and straight, and ended with a sharp edge like a chisel. *Moschops* could easily bite tough leaves and twigs off bushes.

▶ As well as sharp teeth, *Moschops* had very strong skull bones, so it may have head-butted rivals in fights.

Reptiles take over

34 Reptiles don't like to be too hot, or too cold. Otherwise they may overheat, or be too cold to move. Most reptiles bask in sunshine to get warm, then stay in the shade. *Dimetrodon* was a fierce reptile. It had a large 'sail' of skin on its back to soak up heat from the sun.

▲ The name *Dimetrodon* means 'two-types-of-teeth'. It was given this name as it had stabbing teeth and slicing teeth. It measured 3 metres in length.

QUIZ

1. How did *Dimetrodon* get warm?

2. Which types of reptile evolved into mammals?

3. How did some early reptiles swim?

4. Did the first crocodiles like water?

Answers:
1. By basking in the sun
2. Therapsids 3. By swishing their tails from side to side 4. No, they hated it!

35 The first crocodiles hated water! An early type of crocodile, *Protosuchus*, stayed on land. It lived in North America about 190 million years ago. It was one metre long and could run across dry land when hunting, using its long legs.

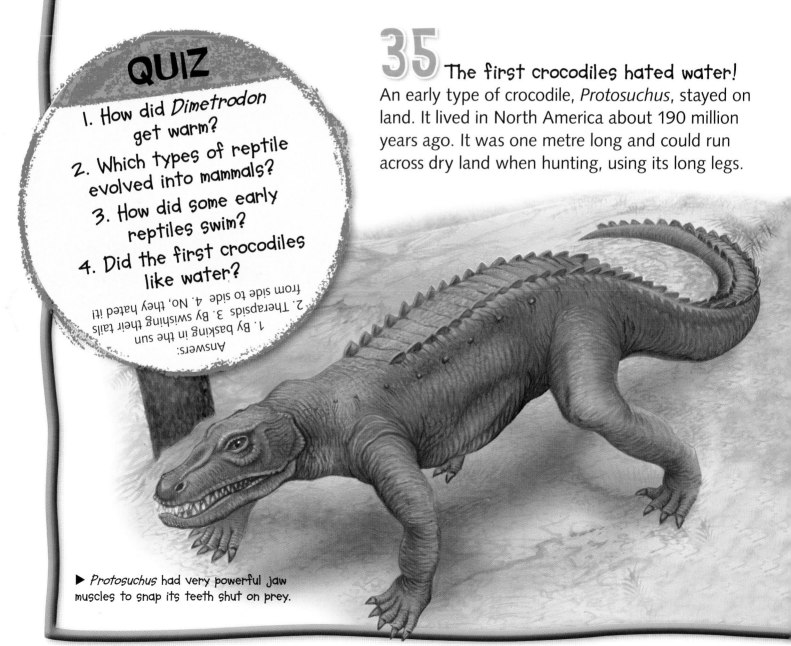

▶ *Protosuchus* had very powerful jaw muscles to snap its teeth shut on prey.

► *Chasmatosaurus* had teeth on the roof of its mouth as well as in its jaws.

36 Some reptiles moved by using their tails. Many types of early reptiles had long, strong tails. They probably lived in water and swished their tails to push themselves along. *Chasmatosaurus* was 2 metres long and probably hunted for fish. It looked like a crocodile but was more closely related to the dinosaurs.

37 Some reptiles began to look very much like mammals. *Cynognathus* was as big as a large dog, and instead of scaly skin it was covered in fur. It belonged to a group of reptiles called therapsids. Around 220 million years ago, some types of small therapsids were evolving into the first mammals.

◄ The jaws of *Cynognathus* were so powerful they could bite through bone. Its name means 'dog jaw'.

Living with the dinosaurs

38 Some reptiles were as big and fierce as dinosaurs – but they lived in the sea. One of these was *Mosasaurus*. It grew up to 10 metres in length and may have weighed 10 tonnes, far bigger than today's great white shark.

39 Fossils of *Mosasaurus* were found in the same place over 200 years apart! The first was found in a quarry in the Netherlands in 1780. The second was found in the same place in 1998.

40 One sea reptile had teeth the size of saucers! The huge, round, flat teeth of *Placodus* were more than 10 centimetres across. It used them to crush shellfish and sea urchins. *Placodus* was 2 metres long and lived at the same time as the first dinosaurs, about 230 million years ago.

▼ *Mosasaurus* was a huge sea reptile. It had razor-sharp teeth and could swim with speed to catch its prey.

▼ *Archaeopteryx* had a long bony tail, unlike modern birds, which have no bones in their tails.

41 Fossils of the first bird were mistaken for a dinosaur. *Archaeopteryx* lived in Europe about 155 million years ago. Some of its fossils look very similar to the fossils of small dinosaurs. So *Archaeopteryx* was thought to be a dinosaur, until scientists saw the faint shape of its feathers and realized it was a bird.

42 Soon there were many kinds of birds flying above the dinosaurs. *Confuciusornis* was about 60 centimetres long and lived in what is now China, 120 million years ago. It had a backwards-pointing big toe on each foot, which suggests it climbed through the trees. It is also the earliest-known bird to have a true beak.

▲ Fossils of *Confuciusornis* have been found in China. It is named after the famous Chinese wise man, Confucius.

43 Mammals lived at the same time as dinosaurs. These animals have warm blood, and fur or hair, unlike a reptile's scaly skin. *Megazostrodon* was the earliest mammal known to scientists. It lived in southern Africa about 215 million years ago – only 15 million years or so after the dinosaurs began life on Earth. It was just 12 centimetres long, and probably hunted insects.

▼ *Megazostrodon* probably came out at night to hunt for its insect prey. It looked a little like a modern-day shrew.

In and over the sea

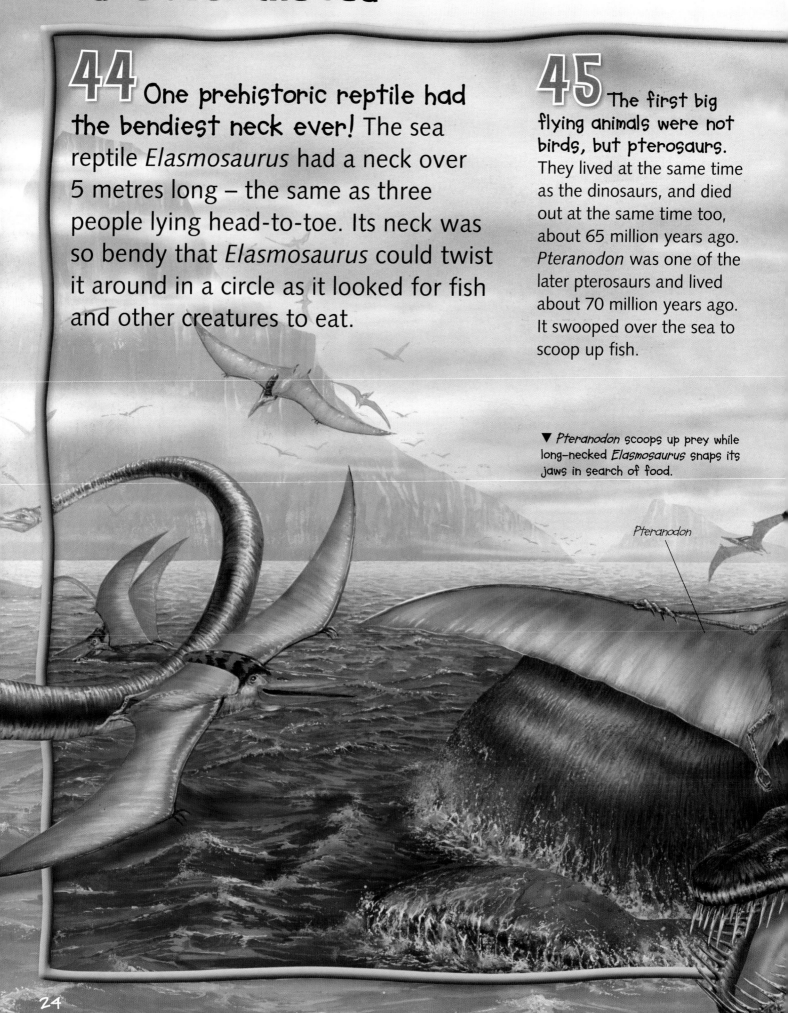

44 One prehistoric reptile had the bendiest neck ever! The sea reptile *Elasmosaurus* had a neck over 5 metres long – the same as three people lying head-to-toe. Its neck was so bendy that *Elasmosaurus* could twist it around in a circle as it looked for fish and other creatures to eat.

45 The first big flying animals were not birds, but pterosaurs. They lived at the same time as the dinosaurs, and died out at the same time too, about 65 million years ago. *Pteranodon* was one of the later pterosaurs and lived about 70 million years ago. It swooped over the sea to scoop up fish.

▼ *Pteranodon* scoops up prey while long-necked *Elasmosaurus* snaps its jaws in search of food.

Pteranodon

46 **The largest flying animal of all time was as big as a plane!** With wings measuring up to 14 metres from tip to tip, the pterosaur *Quetzalcoatlus* was twice as big as any flying bird. It may have lived like a vulture, soaring high in the sky, and then landing to peck at a dead body of a dinosaur.

47 **Some fossils of sea creatures are found thousands of kilometres from the sea.** Around 100 to 70 million years ago, much of what is now North America was flooded. The shallow waters teemed with all kinds of fish, reptiles and other creatures. Today their fossils are found on dry land.

Elasmosaurus

After the dinosaurs

48 A disaster about 65 million years ago killed off the dinosaurs and many other creatures. The main new group of animals was the mammals. Most were small, like rats and mice. *Leptictidium* lived 50–40 million years ago. It may be related to moles and shrews.

▲ *Leptictidium* probably hopped like a kangaroo!

50 Often the name of a prehistoric animal can be misleading, like *Palaeotherium*, which simply means 'ancient animal'. However this name was given over 200 years ago, in 1804, because scientists of the time did not know as much as modern scientists. Later studies show that *Palaeotherium* was one of the first animals in the group of hoofed mammals that includes horses.

◄ *Pakicetus* is the earliest-known whale.

49 Whales began life on dry land and gradually returned to the sea. *Pakicetus* lived about 50 million years ago and was nearly 2 metres long. It probably spent alot of time on land as well as in water.

▼ A mother *Uintatherium* and her baby. This strange-looking creature was the largest land animal of its time. Its head was covered in horns and it had small tusks.

51 Around 40 million years ago, the largest animal walking the Earth was *Uintatherium*. This plant-eater was over 3 metres long and nearly 2 metres tall at the shoulder – about the same size as a cow. Its fossils were found near the Uinta River in Colorado, USA. *Uintatherium* is thought to be a cousin of horses and elephants.

52 An animal's looks can be misleading. *Patriofelis* means 'father of the cats'. It lived about 45 million years ago and was named because scientists thought it was an early cat. Later they realized that it merely looked like a cat. It was really a member of an extinct group of hunting animals called creodonts.

QUIZ

1. What does the name *Patriofelis* mean?
2. How long was *Pakicetus*?
3. In what year were *Palaeotherium* fossils found?
4. How tall was *Uintatherium*?
5. When did dinosaurs die out and mammals start to take over?

Answers:
1. 'Father of the cats'
2. About 2 metres 3. 1804
4. Almost 2 metres tall at the shoulder
5. 65 million years ago

As the world cooled down

53 Before the world started to cool 30 million years ago, palm trees grew almost everywhere — but they became rare. These trees had thrived in warm, wet conditions. But as Earth cooled, other plants took over, such as magnolias, pines, oaks and birch. These changes meant that animals changed too.

▼ *Brontotherium* was somewhere in size between a rhino and an elephant. Males used the Y-shaped horn on their snouts in fighting competitions.

54 *Pyrotherium* means 'fire beast', but not because this plant-eater could walk through fire. Its fossils were found in layers of ash from an ancient volcano in Argentina, South America. The volcano probably erupted, and its fumes and ash suffocated and burned all the animals nearby. *Pyrotherium* was about as big as a cow and looked like a combination of a pig and a short-tusked elephant.

55 Many prehistoric animals have exciting names — *Brontotherium* means 'thunder beast'. Where the fossils of *Brontotherium* were found in North America, local people thought they were bones of the gods. They thought that these gods rode chariots across the sky and started thunderstorms, which led to the animal's name.

56 *Andrewsarchus* was a real big-head! At one metre long, it had the biggest head of any hunting mammal on land, and its strong jaws were filled with sharp, pointed teeth. Its whole body was bigger than a tiger of today. *Andrewsarchus* probably lived like a hyaena, crunching up bones and gristle from dead animals. Yet it belonged to a mammal group that was mostly plant-eaters. It lived 30 million years ago in what is now the deserts of Mongolia, Asia.

▲ *Andrewsarchus* was the biggest meat-eating land animal ever to have lived.

I DON'T BELIEVE IT!

Even if global warming carries on, the world will not be as hot as it was 35 million years ago.

57 Some animals had horns as tall as people! *Arsinoitherium's* two massive horns looked like powerful weapons – but they were light, fragile and made of very thin bone. This plant-eater lived in northern Africa about 35 million years ago. It was almost as big as an elephant and may have been an ancient cousin of the elephant group.

▲ The horns on *Arsinoitherium's* head were hollow and may have been used to make mating calls.

What fossils tell us

58 Fossils are the remains of animals or plants that have been preserved in rock. Usually only the hard parts of an animal, such as teeth or bones, are preserved in this way. Trilobites had a tough, outer skeleton so usually only this part of their body is found as a fossil. Scientists use the fossil to try to create a picture of how the soft parts, such as muscles and organs, may have looked.

▼ Some early humans are known only from their fossil footprints, not from fossils of their bones. These footprints were discovered in 1978 in Tanzania, Africa.

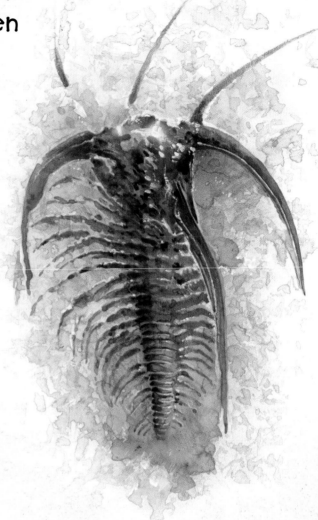

▲ By examining trilobite fossils, scientists were able to tell that this animal could see in all directions.

59 Some fossils are known as trace fossils. These are not fossilized parts of an animal's body, such as bones, but preserved marks left behind by the animal, such as footprints or droppings. By studying the fossilized footprints of an extinct animal, scientists can discover how it walked, how fast it could move and whether it lived alone or in groups.

60

On rare occasions the softer parts of an animal may be preserved as well as the hard parts. Insects may become trapped in sticky sap oozing from pine trees. This sap may then become fossilized as amber, with the insect caught inside. Scientists have found hundreds of insects, spiders and other small creatures perfectly preserved in this way.

▲ Amber spider fossils show that spiders have changed little over the last 30 million years.

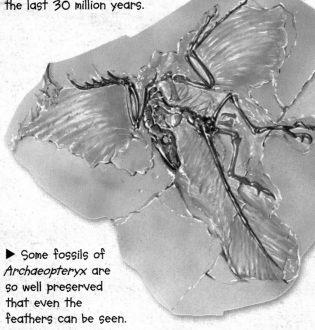

► Some fossils of *Archaeopteryx* are so well preserved that even the feathers can be seen.

QUIZ

1. What is a fossil?
2. What could scientists tell from trilobite fossils?
3. What is amber?
4. What animals did *Archaeopteryx* look like?

Answers:
1. Remains of animals or plants preserved in rock 2. That they could see in all directions 3. Fossil tree sap 4. A bird and a dinosaur

61

One of the most important and valuable fossils ever found was of *Archaeopteryx*, in Germany in 1860. The fossil is about 150 million years old and shows a creature that looked part dinosaur and part bird. It had the feathers and wings of a bird, but the teeth and bony tail of a dinosaur. This shows that birds probably evolved from a type of dinosaur.

62

The importance of some fossils can be misunderstood. *Acanthostega* was one of the very earliest amphibian fossils ever found. However, the man who found the fossil was not an expert on amphibians. When his expedition returned from Greenland, the fossil was put in a drawer at a museum. It was not until over 30 years later that an expert on amphibians happened to see the fossil and realized how important it was.

Prehistoric prowlers

63 Some animals probably ate just about anything. Entelodonts were pig-like animals that lived about 25 million years ago. *Dinohyus* was one of the largest entelodonts. Its teeth were sharp and strong, and it had powerful jaw muscles. It ate almost anything from leaves, roots and seeds, to small animals.

64 Some predators (hunting animals) walked on tiptoe but others were flat-footed. Most mammal predators, such as cats and dogs, walk on the ends of their toes. This helps them to run faster. *Daphoenodon* walked on flat feet, like a bear. It is often called a 'bear-dog' as it looked like a dog but walked like a bear.

▼ *Dinohyus* lived in North America and grew to be about 3 metres long. Its powerful neck muscles and large canine teeth suggest it could have broken bones and eaten flesh.

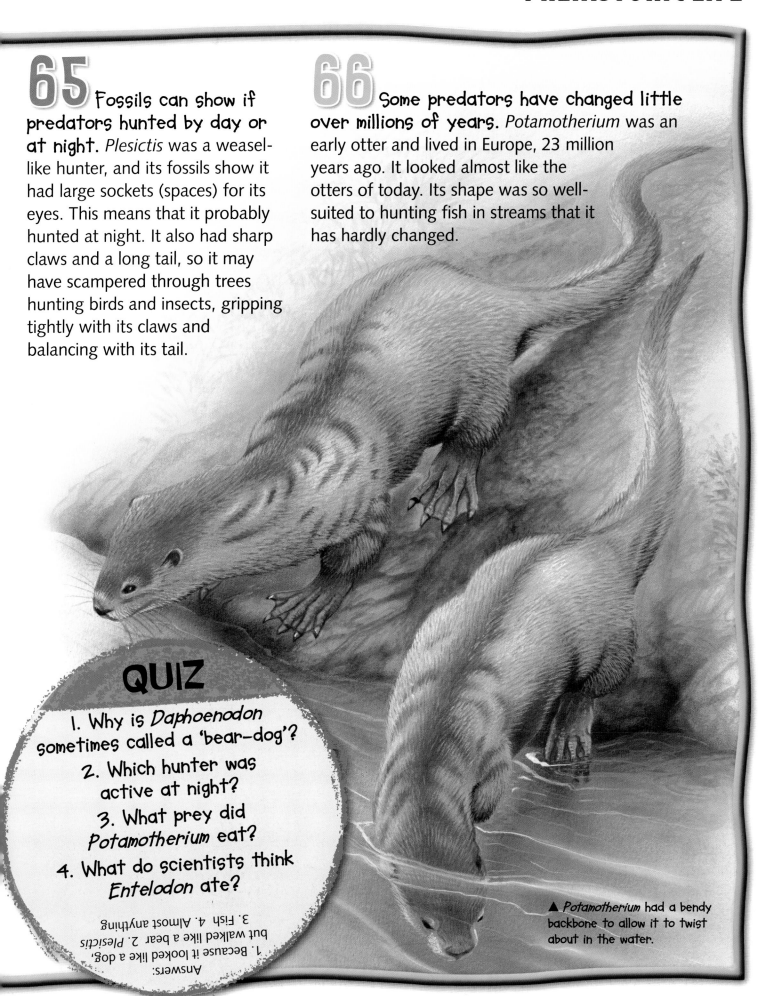

65
Fossils can show if predators hunted by day or at night. *Plesictis* was a weasel-like hunter, and its fossils show it had large sockets (spaces) for its eyes. This means that it probably hunted at night. It also had sharp claws and a long tail, so it may have scampered through trees hunting birds and insects, gripping tightly with its claws and balancing with its tail.

66
Some predators have changed little over millions of years. *Potamotherium* was an early otter and lived in Europe, 23 million years ago. It looked almost like the otters of today. Its shape was so well-suited to hunting fish in streams that it has hardly changed.

QUIZ

I. Why is *Daphoenodon* sometimes called a 'bear-dog'?

2. Which hunter was active at night?

3. What prey did *Potamotherium* eat?

4. What do scientists think *Entelodon* ate?

Answers:
1. Because it looked like a dog, but walked like a bear 2. *Plesictis*
3. Fish 4. Almost anything

▲ *Potamotherium* had a bendy backbone to allow it to twist about in the water.

Amazing ancient elephants

67 The first elephant had tiny tusks and almost no trunk. *Moeritherium* lived in northern Africa about 36 million years ago. It stood just 60 centimetres tall and may have weighed around 20 kilograms – about the size of a large pet dog.

▶ Woolly mammoths had coats of shaggy hair. This hair kept their warm inner fur dry and waterproof in the freezing conditions of the ice age.

I DON'T BELIEVE IT!

The tusks of *Anancus* were more than 4 metres long – almost as long as the animal itself.

68 Some elephants were very hairy. The woolly mammoth was covered in thick, long dense hair to keep out the cold of the ice age. It was larger than a modern elephant and was probably hunted by early people. The last woolly mammoths may have died out less than 10,000 years ago.

69 One elephant had tusks like shovels. *Platybelodon* lived about nine million years ago in Europe, Asia and Africa. Its lower tusks were shaped like broad, flat shovels. Perhaps it used them to scoop up water plants to eat.

71 Some elephants had four tusks. *Tetralophodon* lived about eight million years ago and stood 3 metres tall. Its fossils have been found in Europe, Asia, Africa and America, so it was a very widespread and successful animal.

72 The biggest elephant was the Columbian mammoth. It was 4 metres tall and may have weighed over 10 tonnes – twice as much as most elephants today. It lived on the grasslands of southern North America.

▼ The Columbian mammoth had tusks that twisted into curved, spiral shapes.

70 Elephants were more varied and common long ago, than they are today. *Anancus* roamed Europe and Asia two million years ago. Like modern elephants, it used its trunk to pull leaves from branches and its tusks to dig up roots. However most kinds of prehistoric elephants died out. Only two kinds survive today, in Africa and Asia.

Animals with hooves

73 The first horse was hardly larger than a pet cat. *Hyracotherium* lived in Europe, Asia and North America about 50 million years ago. It was only 20 centimetres tall and lived in woods and forests.

▲ *Hyracotherium* is sometimes called *Eohippus*, which means 'dawn horse'. It had a short neck, slender legs and a long tail.

74 Early horses did not eat grass — because there wasn't any. Grasses and open plains did not appear on Earth until 25 million years ago. Then early horses moved onto them, started to eat grass, and gradually became bigger.

75 Over millions of years, horses gradually lost their toes! The very first horses had five toes per foot, each ending in a small nail-like hoof. *Hyracotherium* had four toes on each front foot and three on each back foot. Later, *Mesohippus*, which was as big as a labrador dog, had three toes on each foot. Today's horses have just one toe on each foot, which ends in a large hoof.

76 Some prehistoric camels had horns. *Synthetoceras* had a pair of horns at the top of its head, and also an extraordinary Y-shaped horn growing from its nose. It probably used these horns to fight enemies and also to show off to others of its kind at breeding time.

▶ The amazing nose horn of *Synthetoceras* was present only on male animals.

▼ *Megaloceros* may have stored food for the winter in the form of fat in a hump on its shoulder.

77 Thousands of years ago, horses died out in the Americas. Spanish travellers reintroduced horses to this area about 500 years ago.

78 Some prehistoric deer had antlers as big as a person! *Megaloceros* means 'big deer' and it was as big as today's biggest deer, the moose. But its antlers were even bigger, measuring almost 4 metres from tip to tip. *Megaloceros* may have survived in some parts of Europe until as little as 3000 years ago.

Cats, dogs and bears

79 The sabre-tooth 'tiger' *Smilodon* had two huge sharp teeth like sabres (swords) – but it was not really a tiger. It belonged to a different group of cats to real tigers. Smilodon's teeth were long and sharp but not very strong. It probably used them like knives to stab and slash at its prey, which then bled to death. *Smilodon* then ate it without a struggle.

▶ *Smilodon* had enormously powerful shoulders, so it may have sprung on its prey and held it down.

80 The earliest cats were similar to those of today. *Dinictis* lived about 30 million years ago and was strong and stealthy, like the modern-day cougar (mountain lion). It probably hunted like modern cats too, by creeping up close to a victim, then leaping on it to bite its throat or neck.

81 The first dog, *Hesperocyon*, had a long body and short legs, more like a stoat or mongoose. It was about 90 centimetres long and lived about 30 million years ago. Only later dogs had long legs and were able to run fast after their prey.

◀ *Hesperocyon* may have hunted in packs. This would have allowed it to hunt animals much larger than itself.

82
The sabre-tooth 'cat' *Thylacosmilus* was not even a real cat! It had a cat-shaped head, body, legs and tail. Yet it was a marsupial – a cousin of kangaroos and koalas. It lived in South America four million years ago.

83
Sea lions did not develop from lions – but from dogs. *Allodesmus* was an early type of sea lion and lived about 13 million years ago. It had strong flippers for fast swimming. Its fossil bones show that it came originally from the dog group.

◀ Early humans had to face many natural dangers, such as cave bears.

84
Early people hunted cave bears, and cave bears hunted early people! The huge cave bear of the Ice Age was as big as today's grizzly bear. Humans called Neanderthals hunted them and used their bones and teeth as ornaments. The bears hunted people too, and left their bones in caves.

Prehistoric giants

85 The largest flying bird ever was as big as a small plane! *Argentavis* was twice the size of any flying bird today. Its wings measured 7 metres from tip to tip. It was a huge vulture that fed on the dead bodies of other creatures, tearing off their flesh with its powerful hooked beak.

▼ *Argentavis* lived about seven million years ago in South America.

86 Some birds were even bigger than *Argentavis*, but they could not fly – and they were deadly hunters. In South America about one million years ago, *Titanis* grew to 3 metres tall. It raced after its prey, which it tore apart with its huge, hooked beak.

87 A type of prehistoric kangaroo, *Procoptodon*, was twice as big as those of today. Yet it could bound along as fast as a racehorse. Like kangaroos of today, it was a marsupial, carrying its baby in a pouch. It lived in Australia.

▶ in South America, *Titanis* was a monstrous hunting bird that chased after mammals such as this early horse.

88 The largest land mammal ever to have lived was a type of rhino – without a nose horn. *Paraceratherium* was far bigger than an elephant, at 8 metres long and 6 metres tall at the shoulder. It weighed over 15 tonnes – more than three elephants. This giant creature lived in Asia about 30 million years ago and was a peaceful plant-eater.

89 Giant marsupials may have started stories of the 'Bunyip', a mythical Australian animal. The Bunyip was supposed to live in swamps and waterholes, and its name means 'devil' in native Australian mythology.

▲ The huge *Paraceratherium* fed by browsing on trees, stripping off the leaves. Even though it was so big and heavy, *Paraceratherium* had long legs, which means it was probably capable of running.

A giant island

90 For almost 50 million years, South America was like a giant island – with many strange animals that were found nowhere else. Until three million years ago, South America was separated from North America by an ocean. On islands, animals can evolve into unusual kinds found nowhere else in the world.

91 Elephants were not the only animals with trunks! *Macrauchenia* lived in South America about 100,000 years ago. It was about the size of a camel and probably had a trunk to gather leaves to eat. It was not a type of elephant, but a distant cousin of horses and rhinos.

92 Armadillos were once nearly as big as tanks! *Glyptodon* was almost 4 metres long and covered in a thick dome of bony armour. It lived in South America until about 10,000 years ago. Today, armadillos are quite small, but they are still covered in bony plates for protection.

▶ South America was once separated from North America. This meant that certain animals that survived there, such as *Macrauchenia* and *Glyptodon*, did not live anywhere else in the world.

Macrauchenia

Glyptodon

93 One South American creature that has died out is the giant sloth, *Megatherium*. It was a cousin of the smaller sloths that live in trees today – but it was far too big to climb trees. At 6 metres long and 3 tonnes in weight, it was the same size as an elephant!

94 When South America joined North America, many kinds of prehistoric animals died out. In particular, animals from North America spread south. They were better at surviving than the South American creatures, and they gradually took over.

▶ *Megatherium* may only have died out in the last few thousand years.

95 The armadillo is a South American animal that lives in North America, too. Over the past 100 years, it has spread north at the rate of one kilometre every ten years.

Our prehistoric relations

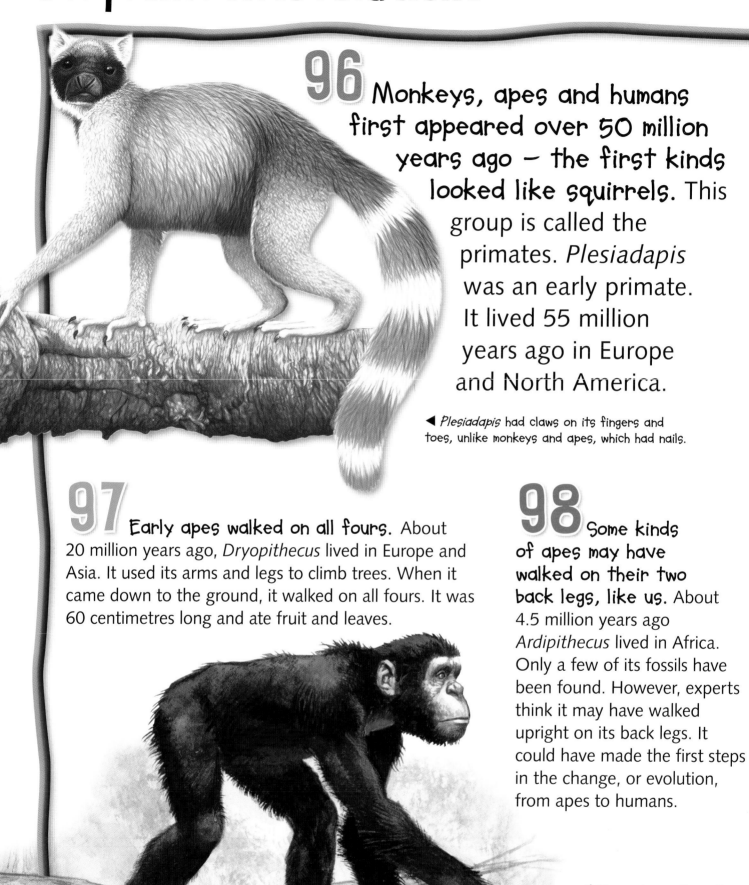

96 Monkeys, apes and humans first appeared over 50 million years ago – the first kinds looked like squirrels. This group is called the primates. *Plesiadapis* was an early primate. It lived 55 million years ago in Europe and North America.

◄ *Plesiadapis* had claws on its fingers and toes, unlike monkeys and apes, which had nails.

97 Early apes walked on all fours. About 20 million years ago, *Dryopithecus* lived in Europe and Asia. It used its arms and legs to climb trees. When it came down to the ground, it walked on all fours. It was 60 centimetres long and ate fruit and leaves.

98 Some kinds of apes may have walked on their two back legs, like us. About 4.5 million years ago *Ardipithecus* lived in Africa. Only a few of its fossils have been found. However, experts think it may have walked upright on its back legs. It could have made the first steps in the change, or evolution, from apes to humans.

◄ The early ape *Dryopithecus* walked flat on its feet, unlike other apes, which walked on their knuckles.

99 The first fossils of a giant prehistoric ape were found in a pharmacy shop in Hong Kong, more than 70 years ago. They were discovered by a German scientist in 1935, who named the ape *Gigantopithecus* from just a few fossil teeth.

100 *Gigantopithecus* really was a giant – it was more than 3 metres tall! Its name, *Gigantopithecus*, means 'giant ape'. It was much larger than today's biggest ape, the gorilla, which grows up to 2 metres tall. *Gigantopithecus* probably ate roots and seeds, and may have hunted small animals such as birds, rats and lizards.

▲ The need to see longer distances on grasslands may have caused the first apes to walk on two legs.

▶ The enormous *Gigantopithecus* could probably stand on its hind legs to reach food.

101 Scientists work out which animals are our closest cousins partly from fossils – and also from chemicals. The chemical called DNA contains genes, which are instructions for how living things grow and work. The living animals with DNA most similar to ours are the great apes, chimpanzees and gorillas, both from Africa. So our ancient cousins were probably apes like them. The orang-utan, from Southeast Asia, is less similar.

DINOSAURS

102 For more than 160 million years, dinosaurs ruled the land. There were many different kinds – huge and tiny, tall and short, slim and bulky, fast and slow, with fierce sharp-toothed meat-eaters and peacefully munching plant-eaters. Then a great disaster ended their rule.

▼ In South America 70 million years ago, a group of *Austroraptor* dinosaurs attack a huge plant-eater. Many fast, fierce 'raptor' dinosaurs had feathers. *Austroraptor* was one of the largest raptors at 300-plus kilograms and 5 metres long.

When were dinosaurs alive?

103 The Age of Dinosaurs lasted from about 230 million to 65 million years ago, during a time called the Mesozoic Era. Dinosaurs were the main creatures on land for 80 times longer than people have been on Earth!

▼ Towards the end of the Palaeozoic Era, reptiles replaced amphibians as the main large land animals. Dinosaurs were in turn replaced in the Cenozoic Era by mammals. MYA means million years ago.

104 Dinosaurs were not the only animals living in the Mesozoic Era. There were many other kinds such as insects, spiders, shellfish, fish, scurrying lizards, crocodiles and furry mammals.

105 There were different shapes and sizes of dinosaurs. Some were small enough to hold in your hand. Others were bigger than a house!

◄ Tiny *Saltopus*, less than one metre long, was a Triassic close cousin of dinosaurs.

PALAEOZOIC ERA

The reptiles, including the ancestors of the dinosaurs, start to become more dominant than the amphibians.

Lystrosaurus (amphibian)

Diplocaulus (mammal-like reptile)

**299–251 MYA
PERMIAN PERIOD**

MESOZOIC ERA

The first true dinosaurs appear. These are small two-legged carnivores (meat-eaters), and larger herbivores, or plant-eaters.

Procompsognathus

Riojasaurus

**251–200 MYA
TRIASSIC PERIOD**

Many different dinosaurs lived at this time, including the giant plant-eaters such as *Barosaurus*.

Barosaurus

Allosaurus

**200–145.5 MYA
JURASSIC PERIOD**

◀ *Stegosaurus* thrived during the late Jurassic Period, in North America and Europe.

107

There were no people during the Age of Dinosaurs. There was a gap of more than 60 million years between the last dinosaurs and the first humans.

106

No single kind of dinosaur survived for all of the Mesozoic Era. Many different types came and went. Some lasted for less than a million years. Other kinds, like *Stegosaurus*, kept going for many millions of years.

I DON'T BELIEVE IT!

The name 'dinosaur' means 'terrible lizard'. But dinosaurs weren't lizards, and not all dinosaurs were terrible. Small plant-eating dinosaurs were about as 'terrible' as today's sheep!

MESOZOIC ERA

During the last part of the Age of Dinosaurs, both giant carnivores and armoured herbivores were alive.

Tyrannosaurus rex

Deinonychus

Saltasaurus

Spinosaurus

**145.5–65.5 MYA
CRETACEOUS PERIOD**

CENOZOIC ERA

The dinosaurs have died out, and large mammals soon take over the land.

Megacerops herbivorous mammal

Nesodon herbivorous mammal

**65.5–23 MYA
PALEOGENE PERIOD**

Newer kinds of mammals become more common, such as cats, horses, whales and bats.

Thylacosmilus carnivorous mammal

**23–2.6 MYA
NEOGENE PERIOD**

Before the dinosaurs

108 Dinosaurs were not the first animals on Earth. Many other kinds of creatures lived before them, including different types of reptiles – the group that includes dinosaurs.

▶ *Erythrosuchus* was a crocodile–like reptile that lived before dinosaurs were common.

109 *Dimetrodon* was a fierce, meat-eating reptile. Although it looked like a dinosaur it wasn't one. It lived 270 million years ago, well before the dinosaurs arrived. Dimetrodon was about 3 metres long and had a tall flap of skin like a sail on its back.

▶ *Dimetrodon's* legs sprawled sideways from its body, like a lizard, rather than being underneath, as in dinosaurs.

110 Early crocodiles also looked like dinosaurs. Crocodiles were around even before the first dinosaurs. One was *Erythrosuchus*, which was 4.5 metres long, lived 240 million years ago, lurked in swamps and ate fish.

111 Therapsids were around before the dinosaurs, and they also lived alongside the early dinosaurs. They were mammal-like reptiles because they didn't have scaly skin like most reptiles. Instead they had furry or hairy skin like mammals.

112 The dinosaur group probably appeared 238–232 million years ago. Lack of fossils means no one is sure when, where, or what were the ancestors. However it is known that the dinosaurs' closest relations include crocodiles and the flying reptiles called pterosaurs, all making up the bigger group termed archosaurs.

▶ *Euparkeria* could probably rear up to run on just its two rear legs – like many meat-eating dinosaurs later.

113 Some small reptiles show what the dinosaurs' ancestors could have looked like. They include *Euparkeria* in South Africa 245 million years ago, and *Lagosuchus* and *Marasuchus* in South America around 235 million years ago. They were small, light and fast, with long back legs, and sharp teeth for feeding on bugs and small creatures.

Dinosaurs arrive

114 The earliest dinosaurs stalked the Earth almost 230 million years ago. They lived in what is now Argentina, in South America. They included *Eoraptor* and *Herrerasaurus*. Both were slim and fast creatures. They could stand almost upright and run on their two rear legs. Few other animals of the time could run upright like this, on legs that were straight below their bodies. Most other animals had legs that stuck out sideways.

ACTUAL SIZE

▲ The teeth of *Eoraptor* were suited to eating both small animal prey and soft plant foods.

The long tail balanced the head and body over the rear legs

Large head with powerful jaws contained saw-edged teeth

▲ *Herrerasaurus* was about 3 metres long from nose to tail. It was small, light and fast.

Each foot had three long central toes with sharp claws, and a smaller, shorter toe to each side of these

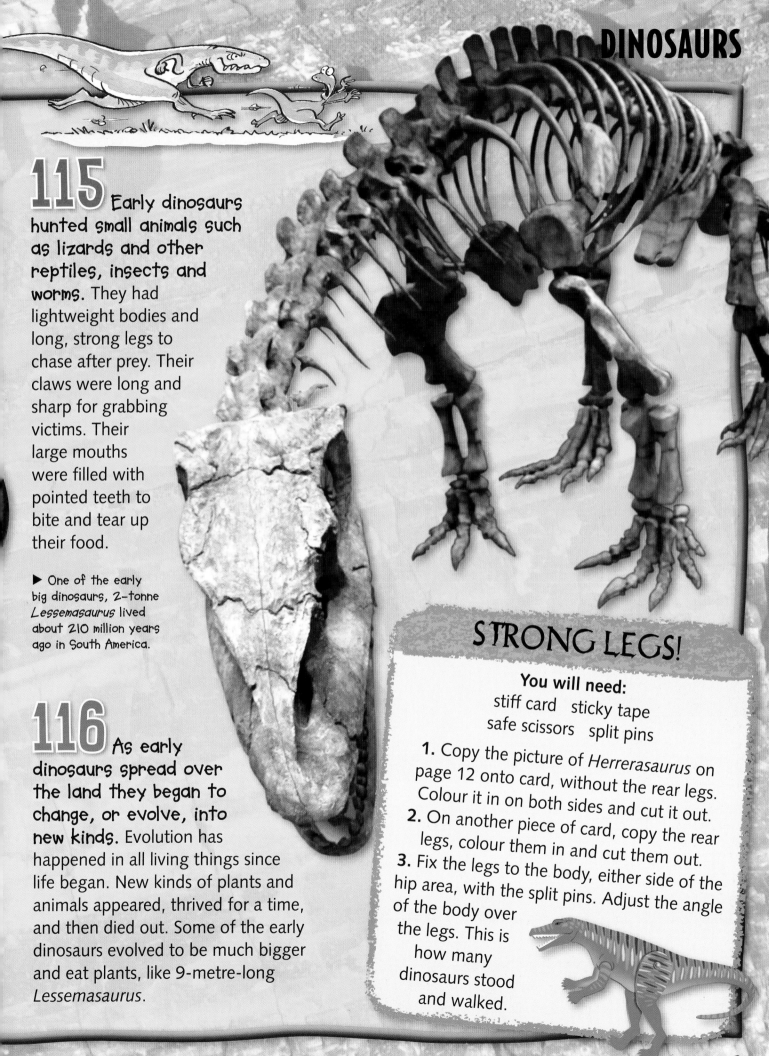

115 Early dinosaurs hunted small animals such as lizards and other reptiles, insects and worms. They had lightweight bodies and long, strong legs to chase after prey. Their claws were long and sharp for grabbing victims. Their large mouths were filled with pointed teeth to bite and tear up their food.

▶ One of the early big dinosaurs, 2-tonne *Lessemasaurus* lived about 210 million years ago in South America.

116 As early dinosaurs spread over the land they began to change, or evolve, into new kinds. Evolution has happened in all living things since life began. New kinds of plants and animals appeared, thrived for a time, and then died out. Some of the early dinosaurs evolved to be much bigger and eat plants, like 9-metre-long *Lessemasaurus*.

STRONG LEGS!

You will need:
stiff card   sticky tape
safe scissors   split pins

1. Copy the picture of *Herrerasaurus* on page 12 onto card, without the rear legs. Colour it in on both sides and cut it out.
2. On another piece of card, copy the rear legs, colour them in and cut them out.
3. Fix the legs to the body, either side of the hip area, with the split pins. Adjust the angle of the body over the legs. This is how many dinosaurs stood and walked.

First of the giants

117 One of the first big dinosaurs well-known from fossils was *Plateosaurus*. This plant-eater grew up to 8 metres long and lived almost 220 million years ago in what is now Europe. It could rear up on its back legs and use its long neck to reach food high in trees.

Long, flexible neck for reaching food high off the ground

Long, strong tail for balance

Sharp, jabbing claws for defence

Powerful back legs for rearing up

▲ Fossils of more than 100 *Plateosaurus* have been found, so its size, shape, teeth and body details are well known compared to many other dinosaurs.

118 *Riojasaurus* was an even larger plant-eater. It lived 218 million years ago in what is now Argentina. *Riojasaurus* was 10 metres long and weighed over one tonne – as much as a large family car of today.

Small head and long, flexible neck

119 The first big plant-eating dinosaurs may have become larger, with longer necks, so that they could reach up into trees for food. Their great size would also have helped them fight enemies, since many other big meat-eating reptiles, some as long as 5 metres, were ready to make a meal of them.

◀ Like *Plateosaurus*, *Riojasaurus* was in the dinosaur group called prosauropods, with a small head, long neck and long tail.

120 These early dinosaurs lived during the first part of the Age of Dinosaurs – the Triassic Period. By its end, 200 million years ago, dozens of kinds of dinosaurs roamed across much of the world.

I DON'T BELIEVE IT!

Early plant-eating dinosaurs did not eat fruits or grasses – there weren't any! They hadn't appeared yet. Instead they ate plants called horsetails, ferns, cycads and conifer trees.

What teeth tell us

121 We know about dinosaurs and other living things from long ago because of fossils. These are usually hard body parts, such as bones, claws, horns and scales, that are preserved in rocks for millions of years. Dinosaur teeth were very hard and formed many fossils.

123 The shape of a dinosaur's teeth help to show what it ate. *Edmontosaurus* was a 12-metre-long duck-billed dinosaur, and had rows of broad, wide, sharp-ridged teeth in the sides of its mouth. These were ideal for chewing tough plant foods like twigs and old leaves.

◀ The head of *Edmontosaurus* was long, broad and muscular, suited to spending hours chewing — similar to today's horse.

Toothless beak-like front of mouth

More than 500 chewing back teeth

122 *Tyrannosaurus* had 50–60 long, pointed teeth more than 20 centimetres long. These were excellent for tearing up victims, and for ripping off lumps of flesh for swallowing. As in other dinosaurs, all through life as old teeth broke or fell out, new ones grew in their place.

▶ *Tyrannosaurus* teeth were strong and stout, but not especially sharp-edged, more suited to tearing than slicing.

124 Some dinosaurs, such as *Gallimimus*, had no teeth at all! The mouth was shaped like a bird's beak and made of a tough, strong, horny substance like our fingernails. The beak was suited to pecking up all kinds of foods like seeds, worms and bugs, as many birds do today.

▲ *Gallimimus* was a type of 'ostrich dinosaur' with large eyes, a long, lightweight beak and long neck.

125 *Baryonyx* had narrow, pointed, cone-shaped teeth. These resemble the teeth of a crocodile or dolphin today. They were ideal for grabbing slippery prey such as fish.

▲ The head of *Baryonyx* was more than one metre long, with an expanded, spoon-shaped front snout.

126 The teeth of the giant, long-necked dinosaur *Apatosaurus* were shaped like pencils. They worked like a rake to pull leaves off branches into the mouth, for the dinosaur to swallow.

DINOSAUR TEETH!

With the help of an adult, look in a utensils drawer or tool box for dinosaur teeth! Some tools resemble the teeth of some dinosaurs, and do similar jobs.
File or rasp – broad surface with hard ridges, like the plant-chewing teeth of *Edmontosaurus*.
Knife – long and pointed, like the meat-tearing teeth of *Tyrannosaurus rex*.
Pliers – Gripping and squeezing, like the beak-shaped mouth of *Gallimimus*.

▲ Although *Apatosaurus* was about 25 metres long, its skull measured just 60 centimetres. It spent most of its time feeding.

Super-size dinosaurs

127 The true giants of the Age of Dinosaurs were the sauropods. These vast dinosaurs all had a small head, long neck, barrel-shaped body, long tapering tail and four pillar-like legs. The biggest sauropods included *Brachiosaurus*, *Mamenchisaurus*, *Barosaurus*, *Diplodocus*, *Futalognkosaurus* and *Argentinosaurus*.

◄ Fossil footprints from a sauropod herd near Purgatoire River, Colorado, USA.

128 Sauropod dinosaurs probably lived in groups or herds. We know this from their footprints, which have been preserved as fossils. Each foot left a print as large as a chair seat. Hundreds of footprints together showed many sauropods walked along with each other.

▲ *Futalognkosaurus*, a type of sauropod known as a titanosaur, was more than 30 metres long. Its name, given in 2007, means 'giant chief lizard' in the local Argentinian language.

129 *Diplodocus* **is also known as 'Old Whip-tail'!** It may have swished its long tail so hard and fast that it made an enormous crack like a whip. This living, leathery, scaly whip would scare away enemies or even rip off their skin.

130 **Sauropod dinosaurs swallowed pebbles – on purpose!** Their peg-like teeth could only rake in plant food, not chew it. Pebbles and stones gulped into the stomach helped to grind and crush the food. These pebbles, smooth and polished by the grinding, have been found with the fossil bones of sauropods.

▶ *Brachiosaurus* was about 25 metres long and probably weighed in the region of 30 tonnes. Its amazingly long neck allowed it to browse from the tallest trees.

131 **The biggest sauropods like** *Brachiosaurus* **and** *Futalognkosaurus* **were enormous beasts.** They weighed up to ten times more than elephants of today. Yet their fossil footprints showed they could run quite fast – nearly as quickly as you!

132 **Sauropods probably had to eat most of the time, 20 hours out of every 24.** They had enormous bodies that would need great amounts of food, but only small mouths to gather the food.

Killer claws

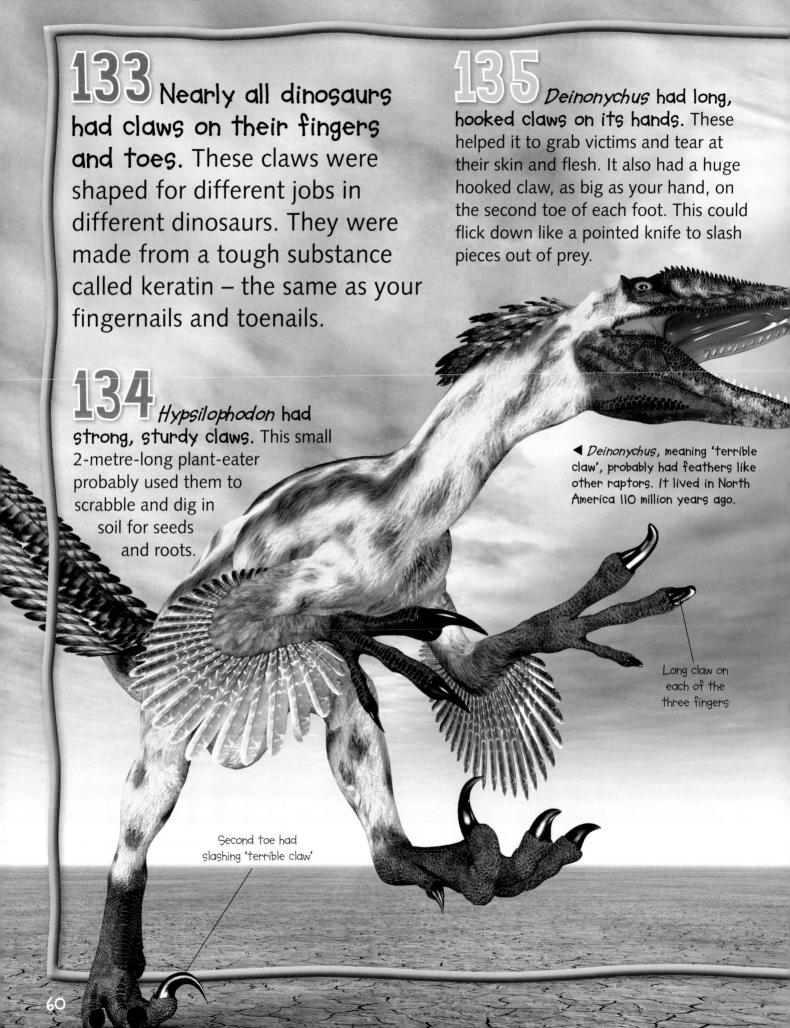

133 **Nearly all dinosaurs had claws on their fingers and toes.** These claws were shaped for different jobs in different dinosaurs. They were made from a tough substance called keratin – the same as your fingernails and toenails.

134 *Hypsilophodon* **had strong, sturdy claws.** This small 2-metre-long plant-eater probably used them to scrabble and dig in soil for seeds and roots.

135 *Deinonychus* **had long, hooked claws on its hands.** These helped it to grab victims and tear at their skin and flesh. It also had a huge hooked claw, as big as your hand, on the second toe of each foot. This could flick down like a pointed knife to slash pieces out of prey.

◄ *Deinonychus*, meaning 'terrible claw', probably had feathers like other raptors. It lived in North America 110 million years ago.

Long claw on each of the three fingers

Second toe had slashing 'terrible claw'

60

136 *Baryonyx* also had a large claw, but this was on the thumb of each hand. It may have worked as a fish-hook to snatch fish from water.

137 *Iguanodon* had claws on its feet. But these were rounded and blunt and looked more like hooves. There were also stubby claws on the fingers, while the thumb claw was longer and shaped like a spike, perhaps for stabbing enemies.

▶ Therizinosaurs, from the Cretaceous Period in Eastern Asia and Western North America, had enormous finger claws — why is a mystery.

138 Giant sauropod dinosaurs had almost flat claws. Dinosaurs such as *Apatosaurus* looked like they had toenails on their huge feet!

▶ The long claw on *Apatosaurus'* front foot was possibly for self defence.

139 The biggest claws of any dinosaurs, and any animals, belonged to the scythe dinosaurs or therizinosaurs. Their hand claws, up to one metre long, were perhaps used to pull down and cut off leafy branches as food.

140 Therizinosaurs were big, strange-looking dinosaurs, reaching 10 metres long and 5 tonnes in weight. They lived late in the Age of Dinosaurs, and the group included *Alxasaurus*, *Nothronychus*, *Beipiaosaurus* and *Therizinosaurus*.

Deadly meat-eaters

Spinosaurus lived about 100 million years ago. It grew to 15 metres in length, and weighed as much as 10 tonnes.

About 13–14 metres in length, Carcharodontosaurus hunted across North Africa 95 million years ago. Its saw-edged teeth were 20 centimetres long.

Giganotosaurus was up to 13.5 metres long and had the largest skull of any meat-eating dinosaur. It lived about 97 million years ago.

141 **The biggest meat-eating dinosaurs were the largest predators ever to walk on Earth.** *Allosaurus*, which lived 150 million years ago in North America, reached almost 10 metres in length, while *Tyrannosaurus rex* from 66 million years ago was 12 metres. In South America, *Giganotosaurus* was slightly larger, while in North Africa, *Carcharodontosaurus* and *Spinosaurus* were even bigger – the largest meat-eating dinosaurs known so far.

I DON'T BELIEVE IT!

Some meat-eating dinosaurs not only bit their prey, but also each other! Fossils of several *Tyrannosaurus* had bite marks on the head. Perhaps they fought each other to become chief in the group, like wolves do today.

142 These great predators were well equipped for hunting large prey – including other dinosaurs. They had massive mouths with long sharp teeth in powerful jaws. They also had long, strong back legs to run fast, and enormous toe claws for kicking and holding down victims.

143 Meat-eaters probably got food in various ways. They hid behind rocks or trees and rushed out to surprise a victim. Some chased their prey, and others would plod steadily over time to tire out their meal. They might even scavenge – feast on the bodies of creatures that were dead or dying from old age, illness or injury.

T rex was among the last of the great predatory dinosaurs. It probably weighed 6–7 tonnes when fully grown.

Allosaurus was the largest meat-eating dinosaur of the Jurassic Period. It was a relative lightweight at only 2–3 tonnes!

Look! Listen! Sniff!

144 Like the reptiles of today, dinosaurs could see, hear and smell the world around them. We know this from fossils. The preserved fossil skulls had spaces for eyes, ears and nostrils.

145 Some dinosaurs, such as *Leaellynasaura* and *Troodon*, had big eyes. There are large, bowl-shaped hollows in their fossil skulls to allow for them. Today, animals such as mice, owls and night-time lizards can see well in the dark. Perhaps *Troodon* prowled through the forest at night, peering in the gloom for small creatures to eat.

► *Leaellynasaura*, was a 3-metre-long plant-eater from 115 million years ago in what is now Australia.

► *Troodon* was about 2 metres long and lived in North America 70 million years ago.

146 There are also spaces on the sides of the head where *Troodon* had its ears. Dinosaur ears were round and flat, like the ears of other reptiles. *Troodon* could hear the tiny noises of little animals moving about in the dark.

147 The nostrils of *Troodon*, where it breathed in air and smelled scents, were two holes at the front of its snout. With its delicate sense of smell, *Troodon* could sniff out its prey of insects, worms, little reptiles such as lizards, and small shrew-like mammals.

148 Dinosaurs used their eyes, ears and noses not only to find food, but also to detect enemies — and each other. *Parasaurolophus* had a long, hollow, tube-like crest on its head. Perhaps it blew air along this to make a noise like a trumpet, as an elephant does today with its trunk.

149 Dinosaurs such as *Parasaurolophus* may have made noises to send messages to other members of their group or herd. Different messages could tell the others about finding food or warn them about enemies.

BIG EYES

You will need:
stiff card   safe scissors   elastic   colour pencils

1. Make a *Troodon* mask from card. Carefully cut out the shape as shown. Then cut out two small eye holes, each just one centimetre across. Colour in your mask
2. Attach elastic so you can wear the mask and find out how little you can see.
3. Make the eye holes as large as the eyes of the real *Troodon*. Now you can have a much bigger, clearer view of the world!

▼ *Parasaurolophus* was a 'duck-billed' dinosaur or hadrosaur. It was about 10 metres long and lived 80 million years ago in North America.

Living with dinosaurs

150 All dinosaurs walked and ran on land, as far as we know. No dinosaurs could fly in the air or spend their lives swimming in the water. But many other creatures, which lived at the same time as the dinosaurs, could fly or swim. Some were reptiles, like the dinosaurs.

151 Ichthyosaurs were reptiles that lived in the sea. They were shaped like dolphins, long and slim with fins and a tail. They chased after fish to eat.

152 Plesiosaurs were sea-dwelling reptiles. They had long necks, rounded bodies, four large flippers and a short tail.

153 Turtles were another kind of reptile that swam in the oceans long ago. Each had a strong, domed shell and four flippers. Turtles still survive today. However ichthyosaurs and then plesiosaurs died out by the end of the Age of Dinosaurs.

▶ In this marine and shoreline Cretaceous scene, the dinosaurs *Ouranosaurus* (4) are shown living alongside lots of other types of animals.

154 Pterosaurs were reptiles that could fly. They had thin, skin-like wings held out by long finger bones. Some soared over the sea and grabbed small fish in their sharp-toothed, beak-shaped mouths. Others swooped on small land animals.

155 Birds first appeared about 150 million years ago. Some evolved to dive for fish in the sea, like gulls and terns today. *Ichthyornis* was about 25 centimetres long and lived along North American coasts.

▲ Unlike modern birds, *Ichthyornis* had tiny teeth in its jaws to grip slippery prey.

Key

1 *Hesperornis* (flightless bird)
2 *Elasmosaurus* (marine reptile)
3 *Pteranodon* (flying reptile)
4 *Ouranosaurus* (dinosaur)
5 *Archelon* (turtle, laying eggs)
6 *Archelon* (turtle, swimming)
7 *Kronosaurus* (marine reptile)

8 *Ichthyosaurus* (marine reptile)
9 *Belemnoid* (mollusc, similar to modern squid
10 *Mosasaurus* (marine reptile)
11 *Elasmosaurus* (marine reptile)
12 *Ammonoid* (mollusc)
13 *Cretoxyrhina* (shark)

156 Mosasaurs were huge, fearsome reptiles that appeared later in the Age of Dinosaurs. Related to lizards, they had a massive mouth full of sharp teeth. Some grew to 13 metres long and weighed over 5 tonnes.

How fast?

157 Dinosaurs walked and ran at different speeds, according to their size and shape. In the world today, cheetahs and ostriches are slim with long legs and run very fast. Elephants and hippos are huge heavyweights and plod along more slowly. Dinosaurs were similar. Some were big, heavy and slow. Others were slim, light and speedy.

QUIZ

Put these dinosaurs and modern animals in order of top running speed, from slow to fast.

Human (40 kilometres an hour)

Cheetah (100-plus kilometres an hour)

Muttaburrasaurus (15 kilometres an hour)

Ornithomimus (70 kilometres an hour)

Sloth (0.2 kilometres an hour)

Coelophysis (30 kilometres an hour)

Answer:
Sloth, *Muttaburrasaurus*, *Coelophysis*, Human, *Ornithomimus*, Cheetah

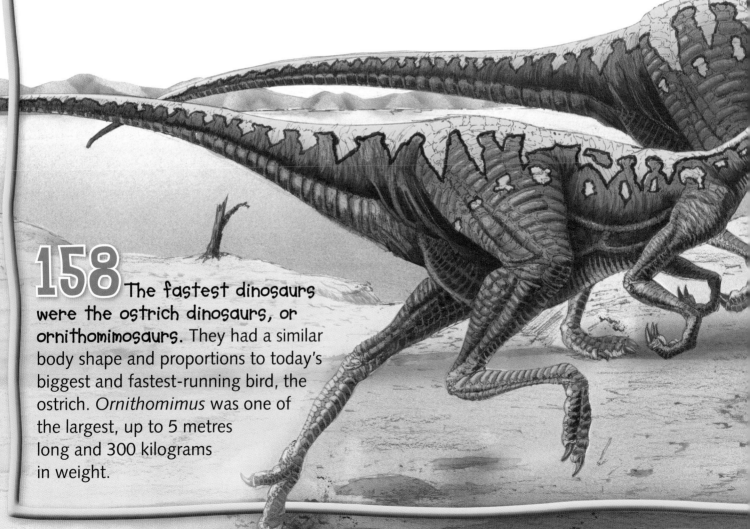

▼ *Ornithomimus*, from North America 70–65 million years ago, had long, powerful back legs, and hollow bones (like a bird) to save weight.

158 The fastest dinosaurs were the ostrich dinosaurs, or ornithomimosaurs. They had a similar body shape and proportions to today's biggest and fastest-running bird, the ostrich. *Ornithomimus* was one of the largest, up to 5 metres long and 300 kilograms in weight.

159

Muttaburrasaurus was a huge ornithopod type of dinosaur, a cousin of *Iguanodon*. It probably walked about as fast as you, around 4 to 5 kilometres an hour. It might have been able to gallop along at a top speed of 15 kilometres an hour, making the ground shake with its 3-tonne weight!

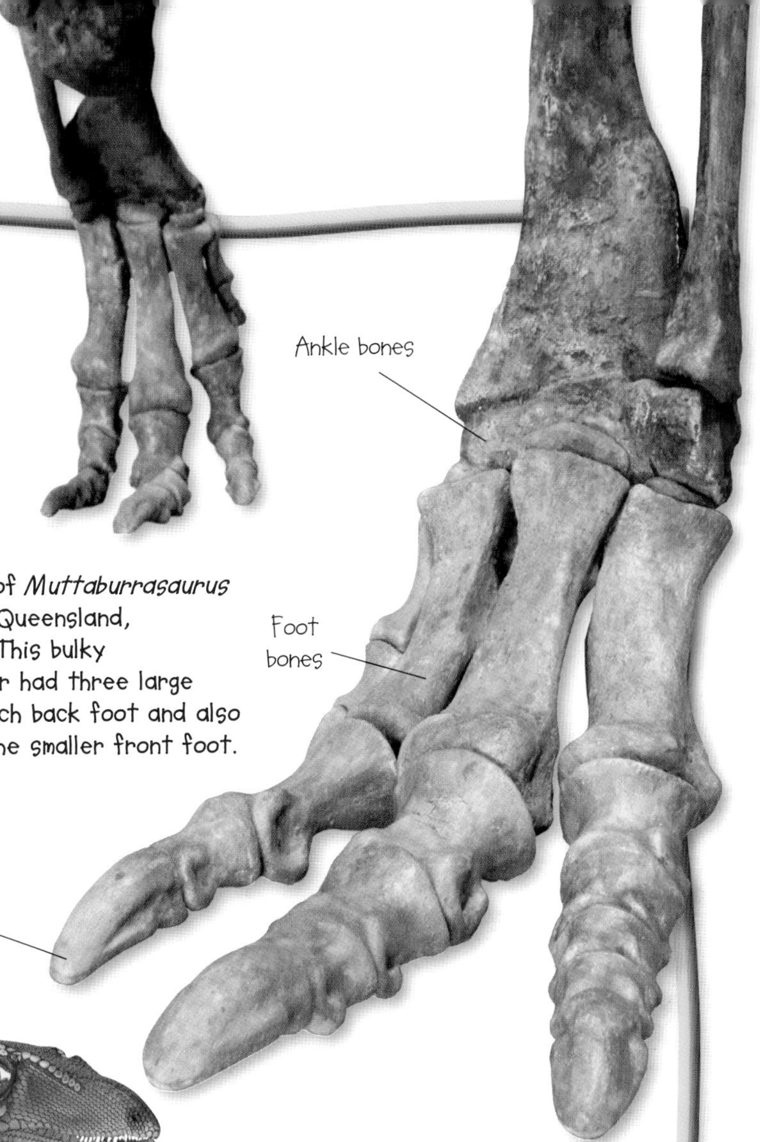

Ankle bones

▶ Fossils of *Muttaburrasaurus* come from Queensland, Australia. This bulky plant-eater had three large toes on each back foot and also three on the smaller front foot.

Foot bones

Toe bones ended in rounded claws

▼ *Coelophysis* was 3 metres long. It was one of the earliest dinosaurs, living about 220 million years ago.

160

Coelophysis was a slim, lightweight dinosaur. It could probably trot, jump and dart about with great agility. Sometimes it ran upright on its two back legs. Or it could bound along on all fours like a dog at more than 30 kilometres an hour.

Built like tanks

161 Some dinosaurs had body defences against predators. These might be large horns and spikes, or thick, hard lumps of bone like armour-plating. Most armoured dinosaurs were plant-eaters. They had to defend themselves against big meat-eating dinosaurs such as *Tyrannosaurus rex*.

162 *Triceratops* had three horns, one on its nose and two much longer ones above its eyes. It also had a wide shield-like piece of bone over its neck and shoulders. The horns and neck frill made *Triceratops* look very fearsome. But most of the time it quietly ate plants. If attacked, *Triceratops* could charge and jab with its horns, like a rhino today.

▼ *Triceratops* was 9 metres long and weighed more than 5 tonnes. It lived 65 million years ago in North America.

Wide neck frill of bone and skin

Long, sharp brow horns

Smaller nose horn

Sharp beak-shaped front of mouth

Wide feet spread great body weight

163 *Styracosaurus* was a ceratopsian ('horn-face') dinosaur, like *Triceratops*, but with a more elaborate neck frill. Up to six horns as long as one metre extended from the frill's edge, giving this dinosaur an even fiercer appearance.

DESIGN A DINOSAUR!

Make an imaginary dinosaur. It might have the body armour and tail club of *Euoplocephalus*, or the head horns and neck frill of *Triceratops*. You can draw your dinosaur, or make it out of pieces of card or from modelling clay. Give it a made-up name, like *Euoploceratops* or *Tricephalus*. How well protected is your dinosaur? How does it compare to some armoured creatures of today, such as tortoises, armadillos or porcupines?

Tail club made from several fused (joined) bones

Long, straight, powerful tail to swing club

Back covered with bony plates set within the skin

▲ *Styracosaurus* grew up to 6 metres long and was 1.8 metres tall at the shoulder.

◀ *Euoplocephalus* belonged to the group called ankylosaurs. With big bony sheets and lumps in their skin, they were the most armoured of all dinosaurs.

164 *Euoplocephalus* had a great lump of bone on its tail. This measured almost one metre across and looked like a massive hammer or club. *Euoplocephalus* could swing it at predators to protect itself from attack.

Nests and eggs

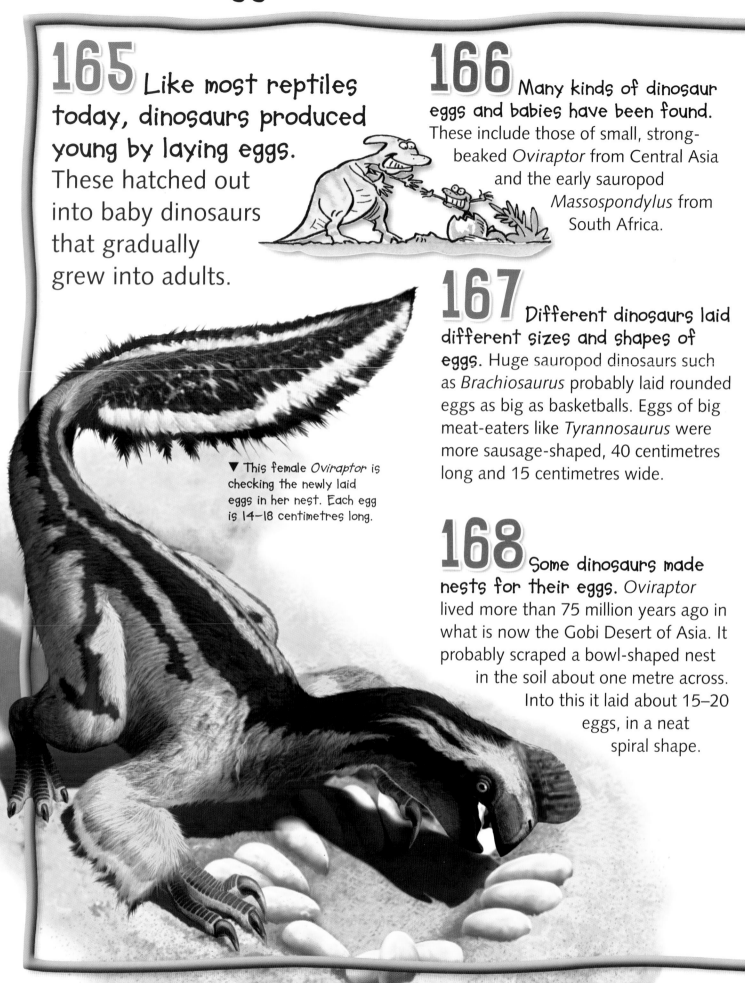

165 Like most reptiles today, dinosaurs produced young by laying eggs. These hatched out into baby dinosaurs that gradually grew into adults.

166 Many kinds of dinosaur eggs and babies have been found. These include those of small, strong-beaked *Oviraptor* from Central Asia and the early sauropod *Massospondylus* from South Africa.

167 Different dinosaurs laid different sizes and shapes of eggs. Huge sauropod dinosaurs such as *Brachiosaurus* probably laid rounded eggs as big as basketballs. Eggs of big meat-eaters like *Tyrannosaurus* were more sausage-shaped, 40 centimetres long and 15 centimetres wide.

168 Some dinosaurs made nests for their eggs. *Oviraptor* lived more than 75 million years ago in what is now the Gobi Desert of Asia. It probably scraped a bowl-shaped nest in the soil about one metre across. Into this it laid about 15–20 eggs, in a neat spiral shape.

▼ This female *Oviraptor* is checking the newly laid eggs in her nest. Each egg is 14–18 centimetres long.

▲ Studying preserved unhatched eggs (real fossil, left) shows they contained tiny baby dinosaurs (artist's drawing, right).

169
Dinosaur eggs probably hatched after a few weeks or months, depending on how warm it was. The eggshells were slightly leathery and bendy, like most reptile eggshells today, and not brittle or hard like the shells of modern birds' eggs.

▶ Seventy-five million years ago in East Asia, pig-sized *Protoceratops* prepares to defend its nest and eggs from a hungry *Velociraptor*.

170
Fossils of baby dinosaurs show that they looked very much like their parents. However the neck frill of a baby *Protoceratops* was not as large when compared to the rest of its body, as in the adult. As the youngster's body grew, the frill grew faster, so its relative size changed. Other dinosaurs' body proportions also changed as they grew bigger.

171
Recent fossil finds show that some dinosaurs looked after their babies, like some reptiles today, such as crocodiles. In one discovery, an adult *Protoceratops* was preserved with some babies just 10–15 centimetres long, probably less than one year old.

Dinosaur babies

172 **Some dinosaur parents may have fed their young.** Fossils of duckbilled *Maiasaura* include nests, eggs and newly hatched young. The hatchlings could not move around because their leg bones were not strong enough. Yet their tiny teeth had slight scratches and other marks from eating food. So the parent *Maiasaura* probably brought food, such as leaves and berries, to the nest for them.

▼ In 1978 more than 200 fossils of *Maiasaura* nests, eggs, babies, youngsters and adults were found at a site now known as 'Egg Mountain' in Montana, USA. They date to around 75 million years ago.

▲ *Maiasaura* was a plant-eater about 9 metres long, belonging to the hadrosaur group. Its newly hatched babies were only 40 centimetres long, but within a year they had grown to 150 centimetres.

173 **The nest of *Maiasaura* was a mud mound about 2 metres across, with 30–40 eggs and babies.** Some fossils show unhatched eggs broken into many small parts, as though squashed by the babies that had already hatched out.

174 Baby dinosaurs grew up to five times faster than human babies. A baby sauropod dinosaur like *Diplodocus* was already one metre long and 8 kilograms in weight when it hatched from its egg!

175 Some dinosaurs may even have cared for their young after they left the nest. *Psittacosaurus* was a 2-metre-long plant-eater that lived 130–100 million years ago in East Asia. One set of fossils from China suggests that one adult was guarding 34 babies when they all died together, perhaps because the tunnel they were hiding in collapsed.

▼ Fossils of *Psittacosaurus* found in 2003 suggest that one adult may have looked after more than 30 babies.

The end for the dinosaurs

176 About 65 million years ago, the Age of Dinosaurs came to a sudden end. Fossils preserved in the rocks show great changes at this time. However the fossils also show that creatures like fish, insects, birds and mammals carried on. What happened to kill off some of the biggest, most successful animals the world has ever seen? There are many ideas. It could have been one disaster, or a combination of several.

177 The disaster may have been caused by a giant lump of rock, an asteroid or meteorite. This came from outer space and smashed into the Earth. The impact threw up vast clouds of water, rocks, ash and dust that blotted out the Sun for many years. Plants could not grow in the gloom, so many plant-eating dinosaurs died. This meant meat-eaters had less food, so they died as well.

178 Many volcanoes around the Earth could have erupted all at the same time, perhaps due to the meteorite impact. They threw out red-hot rocks, ash, dust and poison gas. Creatures would have choked and died in the gloom.

▼ Scientific studies show that 65.5 million years ago, a space rock smashed into Earth near what is now Yucatan, Mexico.

179 The disaster might have involved a terrible disease. Perhaps this gradually spread among certain kinds of animals and killed them off.

METEORITE SMASH!

You will need:
plastic bowl   flour   large pebble   desk lamp

Put the flour in the bowl. This is Earth's surface. Place the desk lamp so it shines over the top of the bowl. This is the Sun. The pebble is the meteorite from space. Drop the pebble into the bowl. See how the tiny bits of flour float in the air like a mist, making the 'Sun' dimmer. A real meteorite smash may have been the beginning of the end for the great dinosaurs.

180 It might be that dinosaur eggs were eaten by a plague of animals. Small, shrew-like mammals were around at the time. They may have eaten the eggs at night as the dinosaurs slept.

What happened next?

181 **Other kinds of animals died out with dinosaurs.** Flying reptiles called pterosaurs, and swimming reptiles called mosasaurs and plesiosaurs, disappeared. Lots of plants died out too. When a group of living things dies out, it is called an extinction. When many groups disappear at the same time, it's known as a mass extinction.

183 Even though many kinds of animals and plants died out 65 million years ago, other groups lived on. Crabs, shellfish, insects, worms, fish, frogs and mammals all survived the mass extinction – and these groups are still alive today.

182 Several groups of reptiles also survived the mass extinction. They include crocodiles and alligators, turtles and tortoises, lizards and snakes. Why some kinds died out in the great disaster, yet other types survived, is one of the main puzzles that experts today are still trying to solve.

1 *Coryphodon* (browsing mammal)
2 *Gastornis* (flightless bird)
3 *Eobasileus* (browsing mammal)
4 *Branisella* (early monkey)
5 *Tremacebus* (early monkey)
6 *Paraceratherium* (browsing mammal)
7 *Arsinoitherium* (browsing mammal)

Key

8 *Hyracotherium* (early horse)
9 *Andrewsarchus* (carnivorous mamm...
10 *Eobasileus* (browsing mammal)
11 *Plesiadapis* (early primate)
12 *Ptilodus* (squirrel–like mammal)
13 *Chriacus* (raccoon–like mammal)

184

After the mass extinction, a different group of animals began to take over the land. These were the mammals. Through the Age of Dinosaurs they were mostly small and skulking, coming out only after dark. Now they could change or evolve to become bigger. Within a few million years they had developed into many kinds, from peaceful plant-eaters to huge, fierce predators.

▼ The mass extinction of 65 million years ago killed big dinosaurs and many other kinds of animals and plants. But plenty of animals survived, especially the mammals.

How do we know?

▼ Fossils form best in water, such as when drowned dinosaurs were washed by floods into a lake or sea.

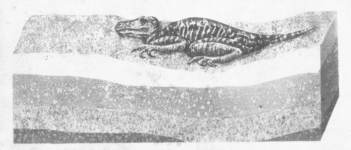

1. After death, the dinosaur sinks to the river bed. Worms, crabs and other scavengers eat its soft body parts.

2. Sediments cover the hard body parts, such as bones and teeth, which gradually turn into solid rock.

185 We know about long-gone dinosaurs mainly from the fossils of their body parts. These took thousands or millions of years to form, usually on the bottoms of lakes, rivers or seas, where sand and mud can quickly cover the parts and begin to preserve them. If the animal died on dry land, its parts were more likely to be eaten or rot away.

186 The body parts most likely to fossilize are the hardest ones, which rot away most slowly after death. These include bones, teeth, horns and claws of dinosaurs and other animals, also plant parts such as bark, seeds and cones.

187 Very rarely, a dinosaur or other living thing was buried soon after it died, then a few of the softer body parts also became fossils. These include bits of skin or the remains of the last meal in its stomach.

▲ Bony lumps in the skin of armoured dinosaurs such as ankylosaurs fossilize well – the softer skin has rotted away.

3. Huge earth movements move, lift and tilt the rock layers so they become dry land.

4. Millions of years later the upper rock layers wear away and the fossil remains are exposed.

188

Not all dinosaur fossils are from the actual bodies of dinosaurs. Some are the signs, traces or remains that they left while alive. These include eggshells, nests, tunnels, footprints, and claw and teeth marks on food.

▲ Dino-dropping fossils come in many shapes and sizes! This scientist is an expert in their study.

QUIZ

Which body parts of a dinosaur were most likely to become fossils? Remember, fossils form from the hardest, toughest bits that last long enough to become buried in the rocks and turned to stone.

a. Skull bone   b. Muscle   c. Leg bone
d. Scaly skin   e. Eye   f. Blood
g. Claws   h. Teeth

Answer:
a. Skull bone
c. Leg bone g. Claws h. Teeth

189

Dinosaur droppings also formed fossils! They are called coprolites and contain broken bits of food, showing what the dinosaur ate. Some dinosaur droppings are as big as a suitcase!

Digging up dinosaurs

▶ At the excavation site or dig, the first tasks are to make surveys by checking the rock for suitable signs of fossils.

◀ Small bits of rock are scraped away. Workers make notes, draw sketches and take photos to record every stage.

190 **Every year, thousands more dinosaur fossils are discovered.** Most of them are from dinosaurs already known to scientists. But five or ten might be from new kinds of dinosaurs. From the fossils, scientists try to work out what the dinosaur looked like and how it lived, all those millions of years ago.

191 **Most dinosaur fossils are found by hard work.** Fossil experts called palaeontologists study the rocks in a region and decide where fossils are most likely to occur. They spend weeks chipping and digging the rock. They look closely at every tiny piece to see if it is part of a fossil. However some dinosaur fossils are found by luck. People out walking in the countryside come across a fossil tooth or bone by chance.

192

Finding all the fossils of a single dinosaur neatly in position is very rare. Usually only a few fossil parts are found from each dinosaur. These are nearly always jumbled up and broken.

▲ After months or years, the restored or 'rebuilt' fossil is complete – this is the skull of *Allosaurus*.

◀ Brushes remove bits of dust, soil and rock flakes. Fragile fossils may be protected with 'jackets' of glass-fibre or plaster.

193

Dinosaur fossils are studied and rebuilt in palaeontology workrooms. They are cleaned and laid out to see which parts are which. It is like trying to put together a jigsaw with most of the pieces missing. Even those that remain are bent and torn. The fossils are put back together, then soft body parts that did not form fossils, such as skin, are added. Scientists use clues from similar animals alive today, such as crocodiles, to help 'rebuild' the dinosaur.

QUIZ

1. What do we call a scientist that studies fossils?
2. How is a fossil 'dig' recorded?
3. How are fossils packed to protect them?
4. What animals can scientists compare dinosaur fossils with?

Answers:
1. A palaeontologist
2. Notes, sketches and photographs
3. They are put in plaster or glass-fibre
4. Crocodiles

Dinosaurs today

194 The name 'dinosaur' was invented in 1842 by English scientist Richard Owen. He realized that the fossils of some prehistoric creatures were reptiles, but different from any known reptile group. So he made a new group, Dinosauria. Its first three members were *Iguanodon*, *Megalosaurus* and *Hylaeosaurus*, all from fossils found in England.

▲ Fossil *Sinosauropteryx* has long legs and feet, lower left. Its tail arches up and forwards to its skull, upper right.

▲ The dinosaur *Caudipteryx* from China had tiny arms and fanned-out tail feathers.

195 From the 1850s there was a rush to find hundreds of new dinosaurs in North America. In the 1920s exciting discoveries were made in Central Asia. Today, dinosaur remains are being found all over the world, even in frozen Antarctica. Some of the most amazing fossils in recent years come from Argentina and China.

196 In 1996 fossils of the dinosaur *Sinosauropteryx* showed it had feathers. This slim, fast meat-eater, only one metre long, lived 123 million years ago in China. Its feathers were thin and thread-like, not designed for flying.

▶ *Microraptor* was one of the smallest raptors ('thief' dinosaurs), just 80 cm long.

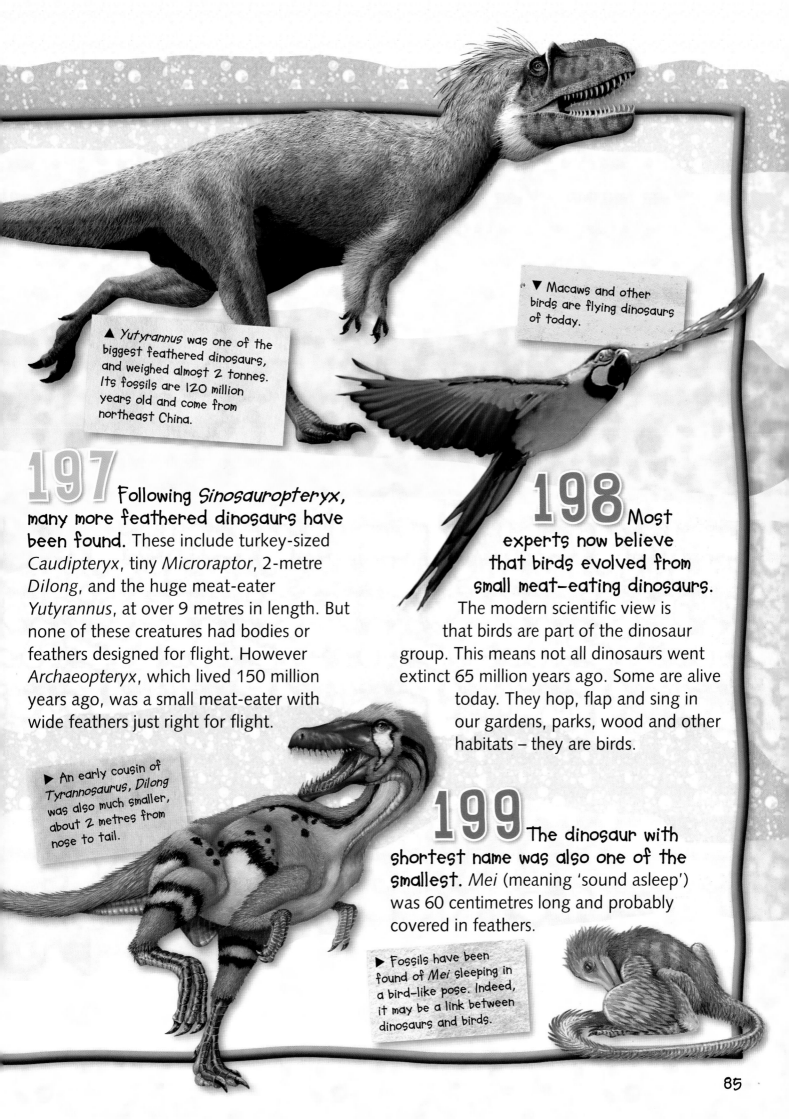

▲ *Yutyrannus* was one of the biggest feathered dinosaurs, and weighed almost 2 tonnes. Its fossils are 120 million years old and come from northeast China.

▼ Macaws and other birds are flying dinosaurs of today.

197
Following *Sinosauropteryx*, many more feathered dinosaurs have been found. These include turkey-sized *Caudipteryx*, tiny *Microraptor*, 2-metre *Dilong*, and the huge meat-eater *Yutyrannus*, at over 9 metres in length. But none of these creatures had bodies or feathers designed for flight. However *Archaeopteryx*, which lived 150 million years ago, was a small meat-eater with wide feathers just right for flight.

▶ An early cousin of *Tyrannosaurus*, *Dilong* was also much smaller, about 2 metres from nose to tail.

198
Most experts now believe that birds evolved from small meat-eating dinosaurs. The modern scientific view is that birds are part of the dinosaur group. This means not all dinosaurs went extinct 65 million years ago. Some are alive today. They hop, flap and sing in our gardens, parks, wood and other habitats – they are birds.

199
The dinosaur with shortest name was also one of the smallest. *Mei* (meaning 'sound asleep') was 60 centimetres long and probably covered in feathers.

▶ Fossils have been found of *Mei* sleeping in a bird-like pose. Indeed, it may be a link between dinosaurs and birds.

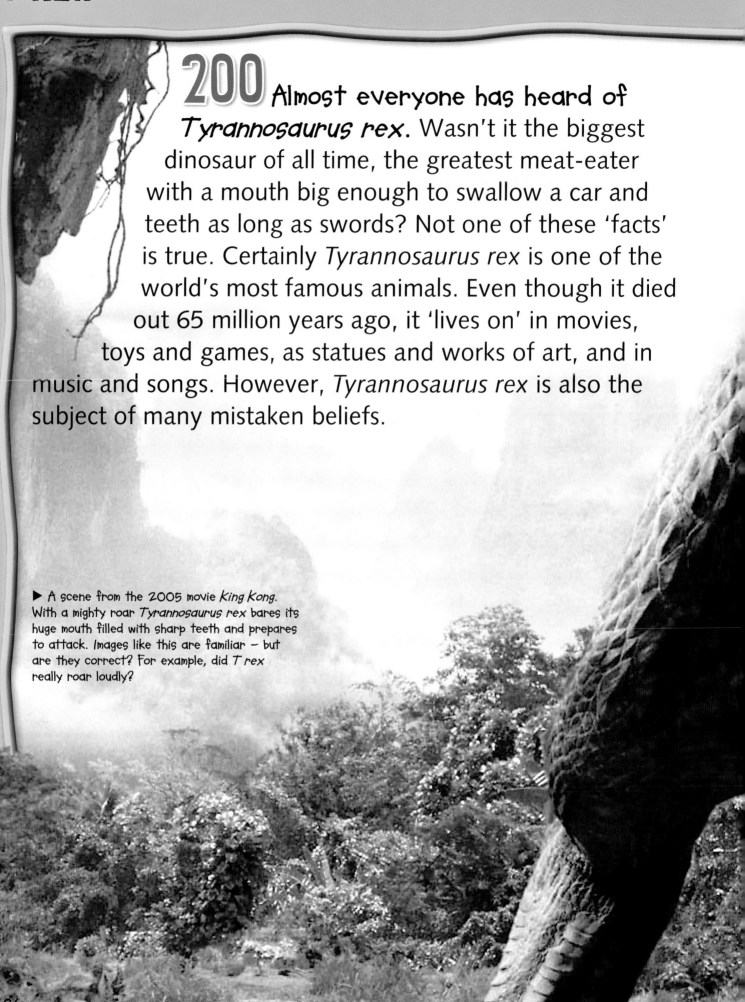

T REX

200 Almost everyone has heard of *Tyrannosaurus rex*. Wasn't it the biggest dinosaur of all time, the greatest meat-eater with a mouth big enough to swallow a car and teeth as long as swords? Not one of these 'facts' is true. Certainly *Tyrannosaurus rex* is one of the world's most famous animals. Even though it died out 65 million years ago, it 'lives on' in movies, toys and games, as statues and works of art, and in music and songs. However, *Tyrannosaurus rex* is also the subject of many mistaken beliefs.

▶ A scene from the 2005 movie *King Kong*. With a mighty roar *Tyrannosaurus rex* bares its huge mouth filled with sharp teeth and prepares to attack. Images like this are familiar — but are they correct? For example, did *T rex* really roar loudly?

Terror of its age

▲ The last dinosaurs of the Late Cretaceous Period ranged from small, speedy hunters such as *Avimimus* to giant plant-eaters, three-horned *Triceratops*, spiky *Edmontonia*, hadrosaurs or 'duckbilled' dinosaurs with strange head crests, and of course *T rex*.

KEY
1 *Tyrannosaurus rex*	5 *Parasaurolophus*	9 *Struthiomimus*
2 *Triceratops*	6 *Lambeosaurus*	10 *Albertosaurus*
3 *Stegoceras*	7 *Avimimus*	11 *Therizinosaurus*
4 *Edmontonia*	8 *Corythosaurus*	12 *Euoplocephalus*

201 *T rex*'s full name is *Tyrannosaurus rex*, which means 'king of the tyrant lizards'. However, it wasn't a lizard. It was a large carnivorous or meat-eating animal in the reptile group known as the dinosaurs.

202 Dinosaurs, or 'terrible lizards', lived during a time called the Mesozoic Era (252–66 million years ago). The first dinosaurs appeared about 230 million years ago and all had died out, or become extinct, by 66 million years ago.

203

There were hundreds of kinds of dinosaurs. *Plateosaurus* was a bus-sized herbivore (plant-eater) from 215 million years ago. *Brachiosaurus* was a giant herbivore from 150 million years ago. *Deinonychus* was a fierce hunter from about 110 million years ago, and was about the size of an adult human.

QUIZ

Which of these extinct animals were dinosaurs?

Pterodactyl
Tyrannosaurus rex
Woolly mammoth
Archaeopteryx   Triceratops
Plateosaurus   Ammonite

Answer:
*Tyrannosaurus rex,
Triceratops, Plateosaurus*

204

Tyrannosaurus rex lived well after all of these dinosaurs. Its time was the last part of the Mesozoic Era, known as the Cretaceous Period (145–66 million years ago), from about 68–66 million years ago. *T rex* was one of the very last dinosaurs.

ERA	PERIOD	MYA (Million years ago)
MESOZOIC		— 70
		— 80
		— 90
	CRETACEOUS 145–66 MYA	— 100
		— 110
		— 120
		— 130
		— 140
		— 150
		— 160
	JURASSIC 201–145 MYA	— 170
		— 180
		— 190
		— 200
		— 210
	TRIASSIC 252–201 MYA	— 220
		— 230
		— 240
		— 250

Jurassic Period: *Allosaurus* was a big meat-eating dinosaur

Triassic Period: *Herrerasaurus* was one of the first dinosaurs

◀ Dinosaurs ruled the land for 185 million years – longer than any other animal group.

A giant predator

205 The size of big, fierce animals such as great white sharks, tigers and crocodiles can be exaggerated (made bigger). People often think *T rex* was bigger than it really was.

206 A full-grown *T rex* was over 12 metres long and more than 3 metres high at the hips. It could rear up and raise its head to more than 5 metres above the ground.

Brachiosaurus
13 metres tall
25 metres nose to tail
40–plus tonnes in weight

207 *Tyrannosaurus rex* was not such a giant compared to some plant-eating animals. It was about the same weight as today's African bush elephant, half the size of the extinct imperial mammoth, and one-tenth as heavy as some of the biggest plant-eating dinosaurs.

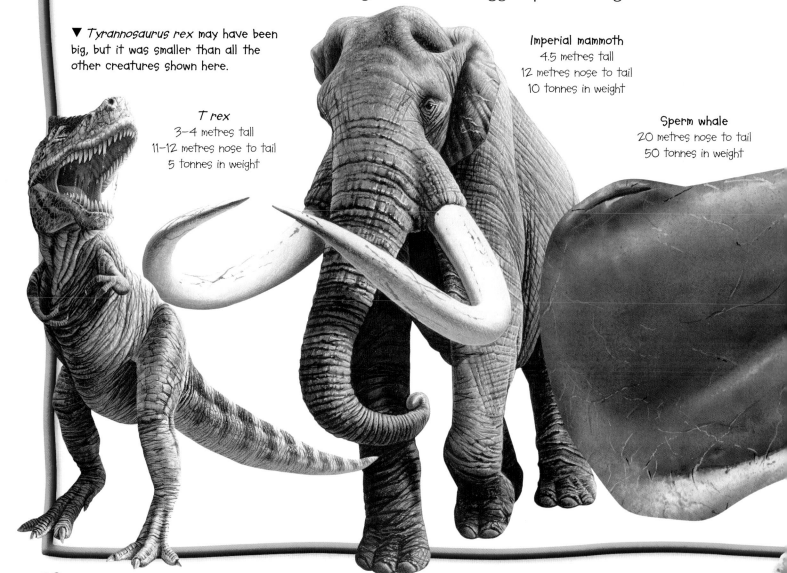

▼ *Tyrannosaurus rex* may have been big, but it was smaller than all the other creatures shown here.

T rex
3–4 metres tall
11–12 metres nose to tail
5 tonnes in weight

Imperial mammoth
4.5 metres tall
12 metres nose to tail
10 tonnes in weight

Sperm whale
20 metres nose to tail
50 tonnes in weight

208 Compared to today's biggest meat-eating land animals, *Tyrannosaurus rex* was huge. The largest land carnivores today are polar and grizzly bears, up to 3 metres tall and over 600 kilograms. However that's only one-tenth of the weight of *T rex*.

209 Compared to other extinct meat-eaters, *Tyrannosaurus rex* was large. The wolf-like *Andrewsarchus* from 40 million years ago was one of the biggest mammal land carnivores. It stood 2 metres tall, was 4 metres long from nose to tail, and weighed more than one tonne.

210 *Tyrannosaurus rex* is sometimes called 'the biggest predator of all time'. However it was only one-tenth the size of the sperm whale living in today's oceans, which hunts giant squid. It was also smaller than prehistoric ocean predators such as the pliosaurs *Liopleurodon* and *Kronosaurus* (10 tonnes or more) and the ichthyosaur *Shonisaurus* (more than 20 tonnes).

COMPARE HUGE HUNTERS

You will need:
pens   large sheet of paper   animal books

In books or on the Internet, find side-on pictures of *T rex*, a sperm whale, a killer whale and *Andrewsarchus*. Draw them on one sheet of paper to see how they compare:

Sperm whale as long as the paper

T rex nose to tail two-thirds as long as the sperm whale

Killer whale half as long as the sperm whale

Andrewsarchus one-fifth as long as the sperm whale

Profile of *T rex*

211 Fossil experts can work out what an extinct animal such a *Tyrannosaurus rex* looked like when it was alive. They study the size, shape, length, thickness and other details of its fossil bones, teeth, claws and other parts.

212 The tail of *T rex* was almost half its total length. It had a wide, muscular base and was thick and strong almost to the tip, quite unlike the long, thin, whip-like tails of other dinosaurs such as *Diplodocus*.

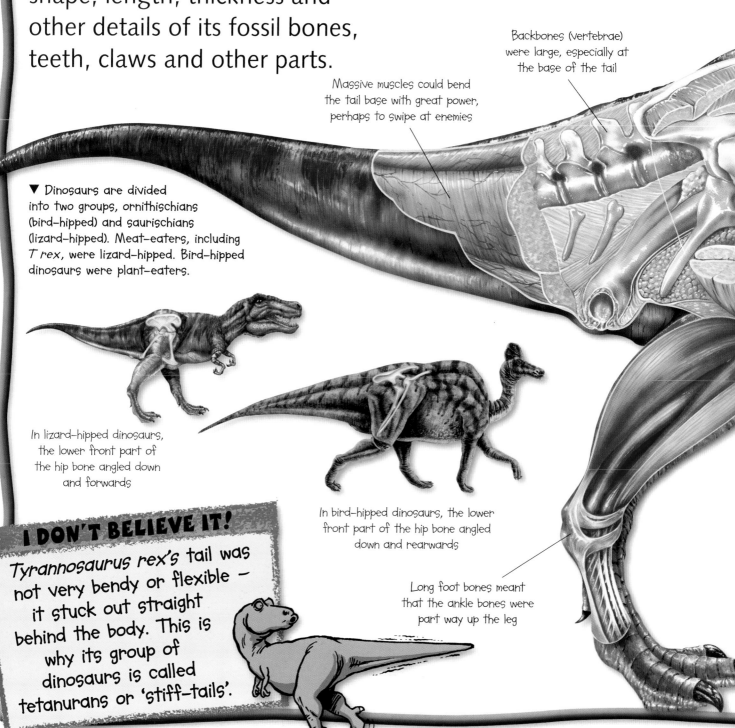

Backbones (vertebrae) were large, especially at the base of the tail

Massive muscles could bend the tail base with great power, perhaps to swipe at enemies

▼ Dinosaurs are divided into two groups, ornithischians (bird-hipped) and saurischians (lizard-hipped). Meat-eaters, including *T rex*, were lizard-hipped. Bird-hipped dinosaurs were plant-eaters.

In lizard-hipped dinosaurs, the lower front part of the hip bone angled down and forwards

In bird-hipped dinosaurs, the lower front part of the hip bone angled down and rearwards

Long foot bones meant that the ankle bones were part way up the leg

I DON'T BELIEVE IT!

Tyrannosaurus rex's tail was not very bendy or flexible — it stuck out straight behind the body. This is why its group of dinosaurs is called tetanurans or 'stiff-tails'.

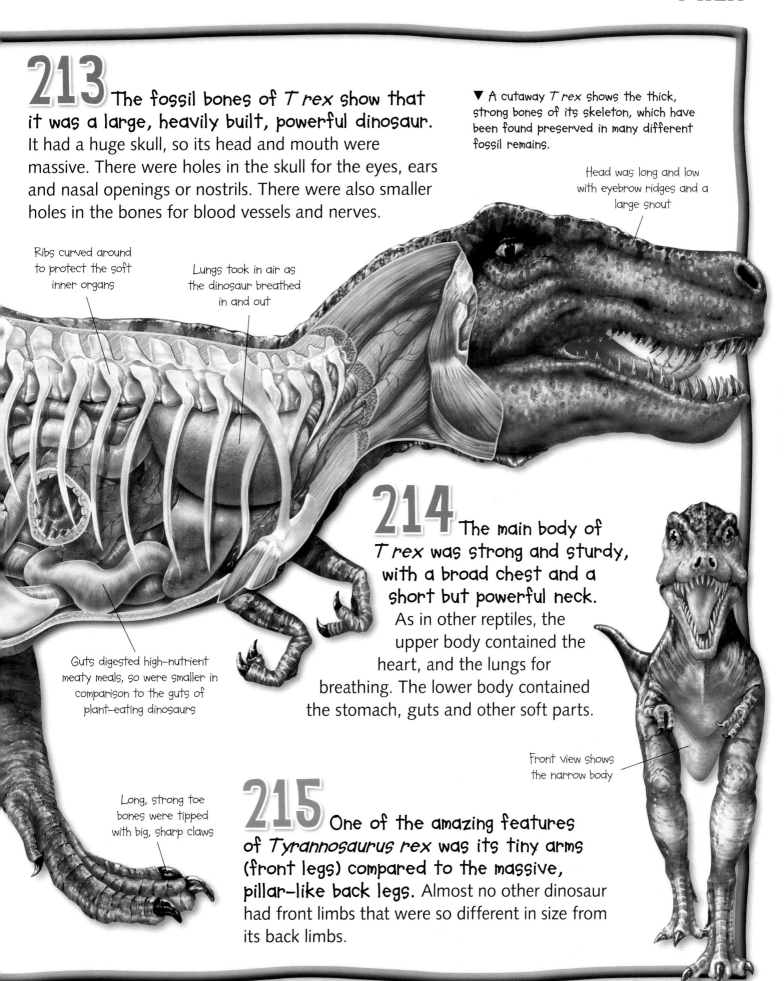

213 The fossil bones of *T rex* show that it was a large, heavily built, powerful dinosaur. It had a huge skull, so its head and mouth were massive. There were holes in the skull for the eyes, ears and nasal openings or nostrils. There were also smaller holes in the bones for blood vessels and nerves.

▼ A cutaway *T rex* shows the thick, strong bones of its skeleton, which have been found preserved in many different fossil remains.

Head was long and low with eyebrow ridges and a large snout

Ribs curved around to protect the soft inner organs

Lungs took in air as the dinosaur breathed in and out

Guts digested high-nutrient meaty meals, so were smaller in comparison to the guts of plant-eating dinosaurs

214 The main body of *T rex* was strong and sturdy, with a broad chest and a short but powerful neck. As in other reptiles, the upper body contained the heart, and the lungs for breathing. The lower body contained the stomach, guts and other soft parts.

Front view shows the narrow body

Long, strong toe bones were tipped with big, sharp claws

215 One of the amazing features of *Tyrannosaurus rex* was its tiny arms (front legs) compared to the massive, pillar-like back legs. Almost no other dinosaur had front limbs that were so different in size from its back limbs.

Was T rex clever?

▼ Many dinosaurs had eyes on the sides of the head, giving good all-round vision but not a detailed front view. T rex had forward-facing eyes.

View from forward-facing eyes

View from sideways-facing eyes

▶ T rex probably used its long tongue to lick and taste meat before it started to eat.

216 The skull of *T rex* is well known from several good fossils. They show that the large eyes were set at an angle so they looked forwards rather than to the sides. This allowed *T rex* to see an object in front with both eyes and judge its distance well.

217 As far as we know dinosaurs, like other reptiles, lacked ear flaps. Instead they had eardrums of thin skin on the sides of their heads so they could hear.

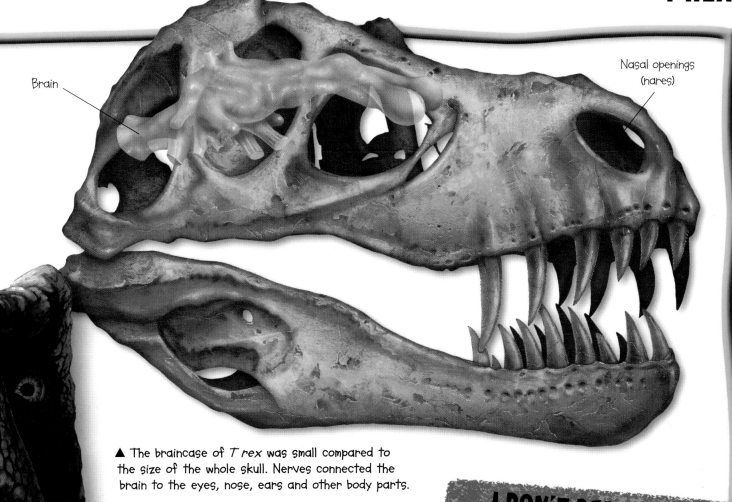

Brain

Nasal openings (nares)

▲ The braincase of *T rex* was small compared to the size of the whole skull. Nerves connected the brain to the eyes, nose, ears and other body parts.

218 *T rex*'s big nasal openings were at the top of its snout. They opened into a very large chamber inside the skull, which detected smells floating in the air. *T rex*'s sense of smell, like its eyesight, was very good.

I DON'T BELIEVE IT!
The eyeballs of *Tyrannosaurus rex* were up to 8 centimetres across – but those of today's giant squid are almost 30 centimetres!

219 Some fossils even show the size and shape of *T rex*'s brain! The brain was in a casing called the cranium in the upper rear of the skull. This can be seen in well-preserved skulls. The space inside shows the brain's shape.

220 *Tyrannosaurus rex* had the biggest brain of almost any dinosaur. The parts dealing with the sense of smell, called the olfactory lobes, were especially large. So *T rex* had keen senses of sight, hearing and especially smell. And it wasn't stupid.

What big teeth

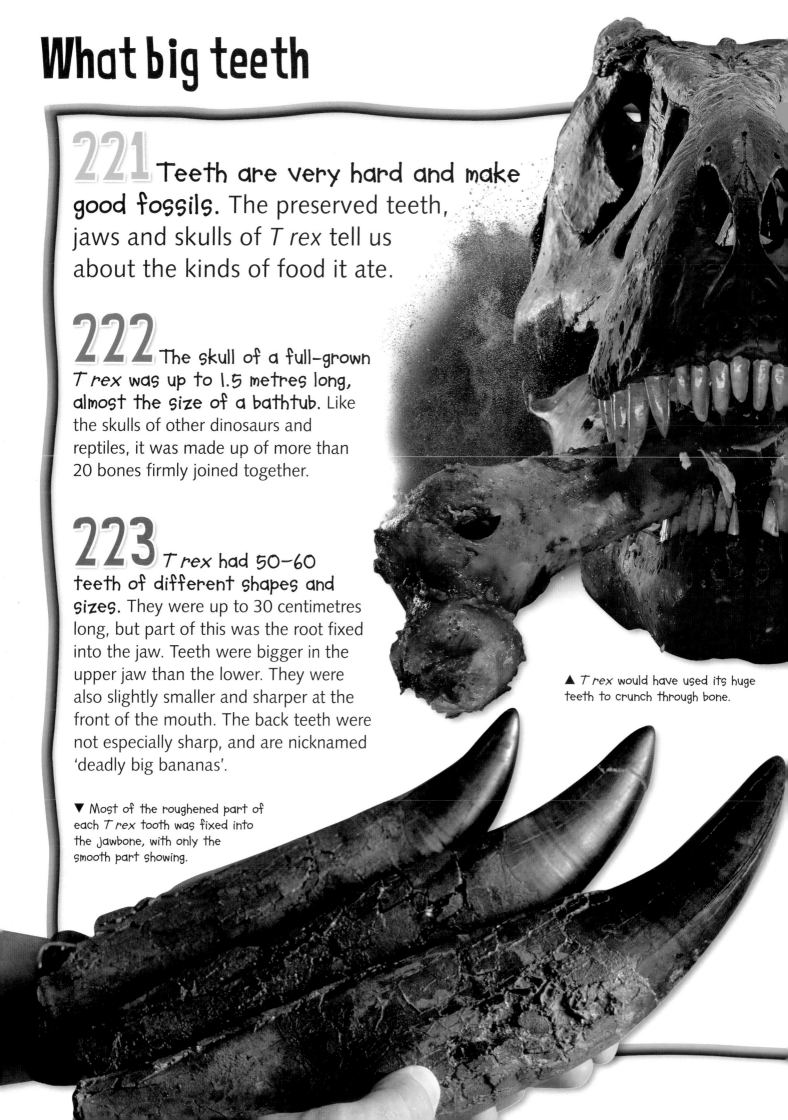

221 Teeth are very hard and make good fossils. The preserved teeth, jaws and skulls of *T rex* tell us about the kinds of food it ate.

222 The skull of a full-grown *T rex* was up to 1.5 metres long, almost the size of a bathtub. Like the skulls of other dinosaurs and reptiles, it was made up of more than 20 bones firmly joined together.

223 *T rex* had 50–60 teeth of different shapes and sizes. They were up to 30 centimetres long, but part of this was the root fixed into the jaw. Teeth were bigger in the upper jaw than the lower. They were also slightly smaller and sharper at the front of the mouth. The back teeth were not especially sharp, and are nicknamed 'deadly big bananas'.

▼ Most of the roughened part of each *T rex* tooth was fixed into the jawbone, with only the smooth part showing.

▲ *T rex* would have used its huge teeth to crunch through bone.

224 *T rex* grew new teeth regularly to replace those that wore away or broke off. This happened in different parts of the mouth at different times. So each *T rex* had a mixture of big older teeth and smaller newer teeth.

T rex

Alligator

225 The jaw joints of *Tyrannosaurus rex* were right at the back of its skull. This allowed the dinosaur to open its jaws wide to take a massive mouthful of food – or perhaps to bite a chunk from a much larger victim.

Hyaena

▶ Because of its huge teeth and jaw muscles, *T rex* probably had a stronger bite than these living animals.

Snapping turtle

226 Scientists' experiments and calculations have compared the bite strength of *T rex* with other creatures alive today. In bite force units, *Tyrannosaurus rex* usually comes out top!

T rex 3100 (estimated)	Great white shark 650
Alligator 2200	Wolf 400
Hyaena 1050	Hyacinth macaw 355
Snapping turtle 1000	Labrador dog 150
Lion 950	Human 120

Great white shark

Tiny arms, big legs

227 *Tyrannosaurus rex's strangest features were its tiny arms.* In fact, they were about the same size as the arms of an adult human, even though *T rex* was more than 50 times bigger than a person. Yet the arms were not weak. They had powerful muscles and two strong clawed fingers.

▶ *T rex's* arms were so small, they could not even be used for passing food to the mouth.

228 *What did Tyrannosaurus rex use its mini-arms for?* There have been many suggestions such as holding onto a victim while biting, pushing itself off the ground if it fell over, and holding onto a partner at breeding time. Perhaps we will never know the true reason.

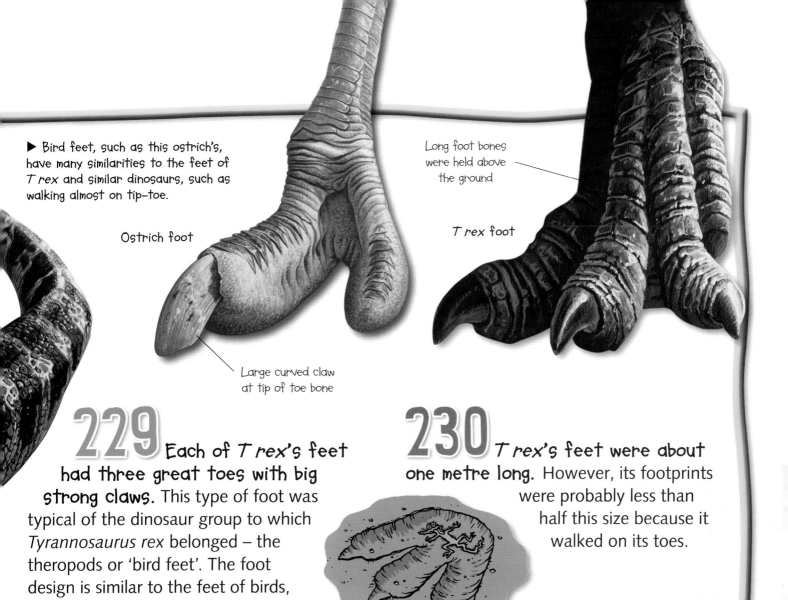

▶ Bird feet, such as this ostrich's, have many similarities to the feet of *T rex* and similar dinosaurs, such as walking almost on tip-toe.

Ostrich foot

Long foot bones were held above the ground

T rex foot

Large curved claw at tip of toe bone

229 **Each of *T rex*'s feet had three great toes with big strong claws.** This type of foot was typical of the dinosaur group to which *Tyrannosaurus rex* belonged – the theropods or 'bird feet'. The foot design is similar to the feet of birds, although much bigger.

230 ***T rex*'s feet were about one metre long.** However, its footprints were probably less than half this size because it walked on its toes.

▲ As *T rex* ran it probably kept its head, neck, main body and tail in a line, almost horizontal or level with the ground.

231 **The big, heavy back legs of *Tyrannosaurus rex* show that the dinosaur could make long strides as it walked and ran.** The three parts of the leg – the thigh, shin and foot – were all about the same length.

232 **Trackways are fossil footprints in mud and sand that give clues to how an animal moved.** There are some trackways that could have been made by *Tyrannosaurus rex* or similar dinosaurs. They help to show how fast it walked and ran.

What did *T rex* eat?

233 *Tyrannosaurus rex* was a huge hunter, so it probably ate big prey. Other large dinosaurs of its time and place were plant-eaters. They included three-horned *Triceratops* and its cousins, and various 'duckbilled' dinosaurs (hadrosaurs) such as *Parasaurolophus* and *Edmontosaurus*.

▼ The giant pterosaur (flying reptile) *Quetzalcoatlus* lived at about the same time as *T rex*. It may have pecked at the remains of a *T rex* kill after the dinosaur had finished feasting.

234 *T rex* could have used its huge mouth, strong teeth and powerful jaw muscles to attack big plant-eaters. It may have lunged at a victim with one massive bite to cause a slashing wound. Then it would retreat a short distance and wait for the prey to weaken from blood loss before moving in to feed.

◀ An adult *Triceratops* would be a fierce foe for *T rex* to tackle. However young, sick and old *Triceratops* might have been easier to kill.

235 One fossil of *Triceratops* has scratch-like gouge marks on its large, bony neck frill. These could have been made by *Tyrannosaurus rex* teeth. The marks are about the correct distance apart, matching the spacing of *T rex* teeth.

▶ The hadrosaur *Parasaurolophus* might have made loud trumpeting noises through its hollow tube-like head crest, to warn others in its herd that *T rex* was near.

236 Coprolites are preserved lumps of animal dung or droppings, fossilized into hard stone. Several large coprolites have been found that could be from *Tyrannosaurus rex*. They show many jumbled fragments of bone from its victims, including young *Edmontosaurus* and *Triceratops*.

▶ Coprolites can be broken apart or sawn through to study the bits of bones, teeth and other items inside.

237 A coprolite found in 1995 in Saskatchewan, Canada was probably produced by *T rex*. It was 42 centimetres long, 15 centimetres wide and 12 centimetres high!

238 In some dinosaurs, several fossil skeletons have been found preserved together, suggesting they lived as a pack or herd. The remains of several *Tyrannosaurus rex* have also been found in this way, which might suggest a family or a pack-hunting group. Some experts say that more evidence is needed for this idea.

▶ Armoured dinosaurs like *Euoplocephalus* may have defended themselves against *T rex* by swinging their heavy, clubbed tails.

Hunter or scavenger?

239 Was *T rex* an active hunter that chased after its victims? Was it an ambush predator that hid in wait to rush out at prey? Was it a scavenger that ate any dead or dying dinosaurs it found? Or did it chase other dinosaurs from their kills and steal the meal for itself?

240 To be an active pursuit hunter, *T rex* must have been able to run fast. Scientists have tried to work out its running speed using models and computers, and by comparisons with other animals.

WHO DOES WHAT?

Research these animals living today and find out if they are mainly fast hunters, sneaky ambushers or scavengers.
Tiger Cheetah Hyaena
Crocodile Vulture
African wild dog

▶ *Tyrannosaurus rex* may have run down smaller dinosaurs such as these *Prenocephale*, perhaps rushing out from its hiding place in a clump of trees.

▲ When scavenging, *T rex* might sniff out a dinosaur that had died from illness or injury.

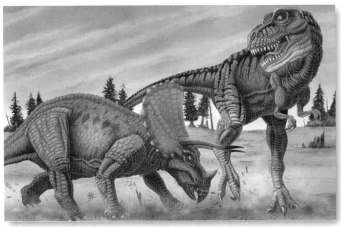

▲ When hunting, *T rex* would be at risk from injury, such as from the horns of *Triceratops*.

241 Some estimates for the running speed of *T rex* are as fast as 50 kilometres an hour, others as slow as 15 kilometres an hour. Most give a speed of between 20 and 30 kilometres an hour. This is slightly slower than a human sprinter, but probably faster than typical *T rex* prey such as *Triceratops*.

242 Several *T rex* fossils show injuries to body parts such as shins, ribs, neck and jaws. These could have been made by victims fighting back, suggesting that *T rex* hunted live prey.

▶ *T rex* would tear and rip flesh from large prey, gulp in lumps and swallow them whole.

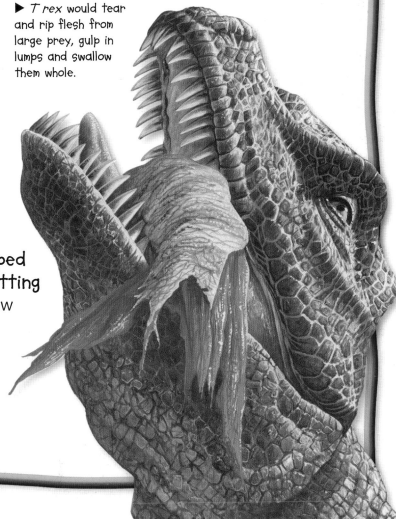

243 Evidence that *T rex* was a scavenger includes its very well developed sense of smell for sniffing out dead, rotting bodies. Also, its powerful teeth could not chew food repeatedly like we do, but they could crush bones at first bite to get at the nutritious jelly-like marrow inside. Maybe a hungry *Tyrannosaurus rex* simply ate anything it could catch or find, so it was a hunter, ambusher and scavenger all in one.

Growing up

244 Did *T rex* live in groups? Most of its fossils are of lone individuals. Some were found near other specimens of *T rex*. These could have been preserved near each other by chance, or they could have been a group that all died together.

Embryo   Yolk

▲ A baby dinosaur developed as an embryo in its egg, fed by nutrients from the yolk.

► The baby probably hatched out by biting through the tough shell, which was flexible like leather.

245 Living reptiles lay eggs that hatch into young, and dinosaurs such as *T rex* probably did the same. Many fossil dinosaur eggs have been discovered, but none are known for certain to be from *T rex*. Some dinosaurs laid eggs in nests and looked after their young, but again there are no fossils like this for *T rex*.

247 It seems that *T rex* grew slowly for about 12–14 years. Then suddenly it grew very fast, putting on about 2 kilograms every day as a teenager. By 20 years it was full-grown.

► Young *T rex* may have killed small prey such as birds, lizards and newly hatched dinosaurs.

246 Fossils of individual *T rex* are of different sizes and ages, showing how this dinosaur grew up. Some of the fossil bones are so well preserved that they have 'growth rings' almost like a tree trunk, showing growth speed.

248 Can we tell apart female and male *Tyrannosaurus rex* from their fossils? Some scientists thought that females were bigger, with stronger, thicker bones than the males. However the latest evidence makes this less clear.

► In many reptiles today, the adults keep growing with age. However their growth rate gradually reduces, so they get bigger more slowly. It is not certain if dinosaurs such as *T rex* grew like this.

249 The biggest *T rex* found, 'Sue', was about 28 years old when it died. No one knows for certain if *Tyrannosaurus rex* could live longer. As with many of these questions, more fossil finds will help to fill in the details.

Where in the world?

250 *T rex* was one kind, or species, of dinosaur in a group of species known as the genus *Tyrannosaurus*. Were there any other members of this genus?

251 After *T rex* fossils were discovered and named over 100 years ago, fossil-hunters began to find the remains of many similar huge predators. Some were given their own names in the genus *Tyrannosaurus*, but most have now been renamed *Tyrannosaurus rex*.

252 *Tarbosaurus*, 'terrifying lizard', was very similar to *T rex*, almost as big, and it lived at the same time. However its fossils come from Asia – Mongolia and China – rather than North America. Some experts consider it to be another species of *Tyrannosaurus*, called *Tyrannosaurus bataar*. Others think that it's so similar to *T rex* that it should be called *Tyrannosaurus rex*.

253 Fossils of smaller dinosaurs similar to *T rex* have been found in Europe. They include the 6-metre-long *Eotyrannus*, from more than 100 million years ago, from the Isle of Wight, southern England. Fossils of *Aviatyrannis* from Portugal are even older, and date from the Jurassic Period.

◀ *Tarbosaurus* had big teeth, tiny arms and many other features similar to *T rex*. It was named by Russian fossil expert Evgeny Maleev in 1955, exactly 50 years after *T rex* was named.

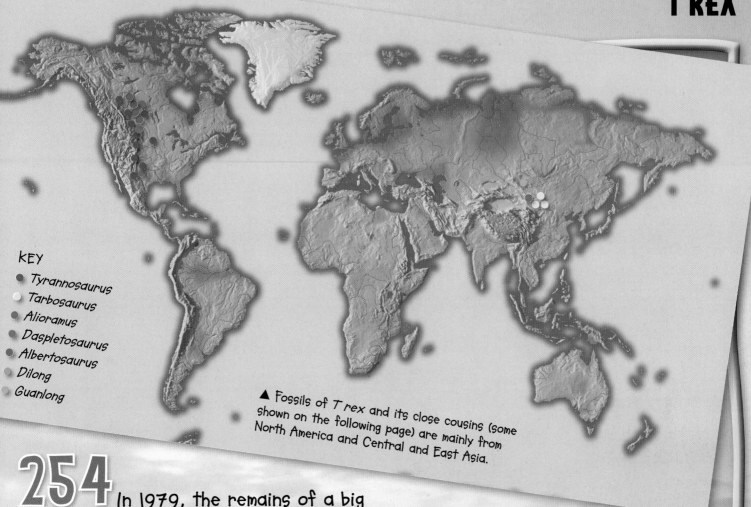

KEY
- Tyrannosaurus
- Tarbosaurus
- Alioramus
- Daspletosaurus
- Albertosaurus
- Dilong
- Guanlong

▲ Fossils of *T rex* and its close cousins (some shown on the following page) are mainly from North America and Central and East Asia.

254 In 1979, the remains of a big Asian meat-eating dinosaur were named as *Tyrannosaurus luanchuanensis*, in the same genus as *Tyrannosaurus rex*. After much discussion another name was suggested – *Jenghizkhan*. However some scientists say that like *Tarbosaurus*, *Jenghizkhan* is so similar to *T rex* that it should be called *Tyrannosaurus*.

▼ Many *T rex* fossils come from rock layers known as the Hell Creek Formation. These are found mainly in Montana, also in parts of Wyoming, North Dakota and South Dakota, USA.

255 A fossil skull found in 1942 was named *Nanotyrannus*, 'tiny tyrant'. It may be a separate kind of small tyrannosaur – or simply a young *T rex*. Experts are undecided.

Tyrannosaur group

256 What kind of dinosaur was *Tyrannosaurus rex?* It belonged to the group called tyrannosaurs, known scientifically as the family *Tyrannosauridae*. These dinosaurs had bones, joints and other features that were different from other predatory dinosaurs. They were part of an even bigger group, the tyrannosauroids.

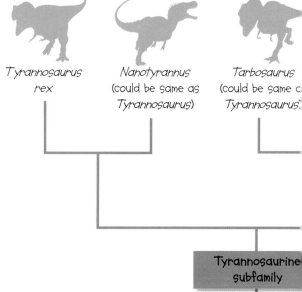

Tyrannosaurus rex

Nanotyrannus (could be same as Tyrannosaurus)

Tarbosaurus (could be same ... Tyrannosaurus...

Tyrannosaurine subfamily

257 One of the first tyrannosauroids was *Guanlong,* 'crown dragon'. Its fossils were discovered in China in 2006 and are about 160 million years old – nearly 100 million years before *Tyrannosaurus rex*. It was 3 metres long and had a strange horn-like plate of bone on its nose.

▲ *Guanlong* may have shown off the crest of thin bone on its head to possible partners at breeding time.

▼ The 'feathers' of *Dilong* were similar to fur and may have kept its body warm.

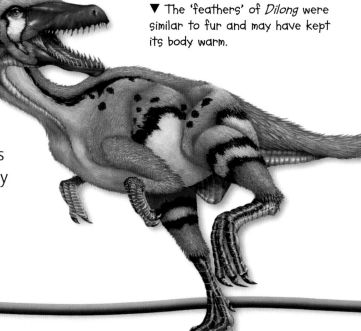

258 Another early cousin of *T rex* was *Dilong*, 'emperor dragon', also from China. Its fossils date to 130 million years ago. *Dilong* was about 2 metres long when fully grown. It had traces of hair-like feathers on the head and tail. As shown later, some experts suggest *Tyrannosaurus rex* itself may have had some kind of feathers.

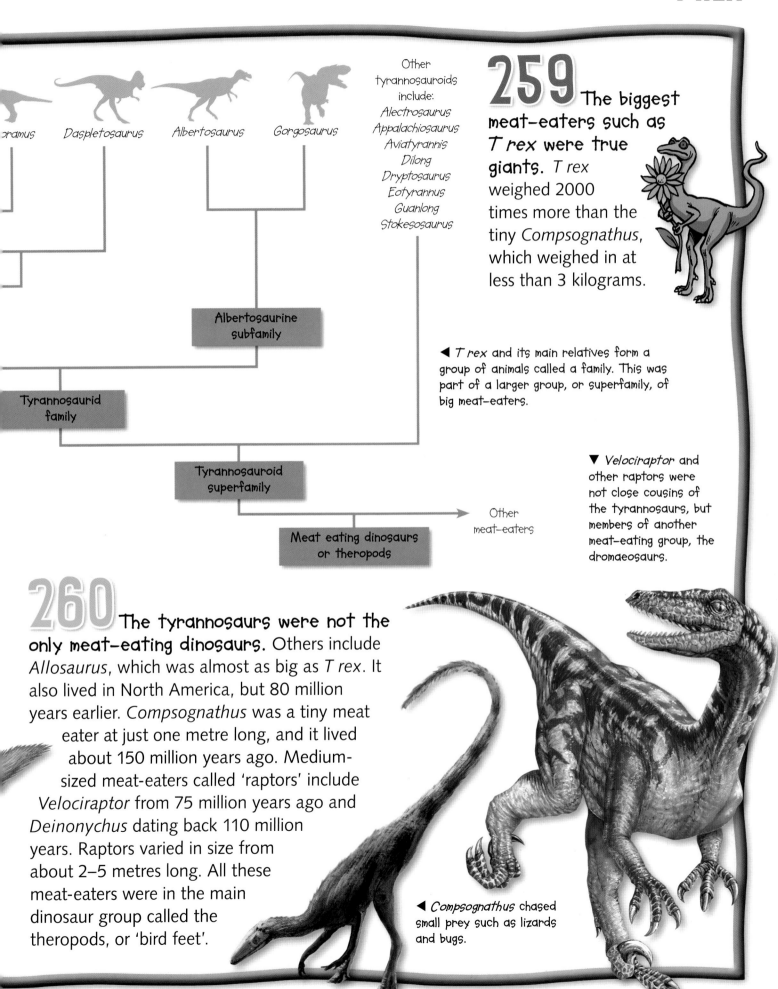

oramus   Daspletosaurus   Albertosaurus   Gorgosaurus

Other tyrannosauroids include:
Alectrosaurus
Appalachiosaurus
Aviatyrannis
Dilong
Dryptosaurus
Eotyrannus
Guanlong
Stokesosaurus

Albertosaurine subfamily

Tyrannosaurid family

Tyrannosauroid superfamily

Meat eating dinosaurs or theropods

Other meat-eaters

259 The biggest meat-eaters such as *T rex* were true giants. *T rex* weighed 2000 times more than the tiny *Compsognathus*, which weighed in at less than 3 kilograms.

◀ *T rex* and its main relatives form a group of animals called a family. This was part of a larger group, or superfamily, of big meat-eaters.

▼ *Velociraptor* and other raptors were not close cousins of the tyrannosaurs, but members of another meat-eating group, the dromaeosaurs.

260 The tyrannosaurs were not the only meat-eating dinosaurs. Others include *Allosaurus*, which was almost as big as *T rex*. It also lived in North America, but 80 million years earlier. *Compsognathus* was a tiny meat eater at just one metre long, and it lived about 150 million years ago. Medium-sized meat-eaters called 'raptors' include *Velociraptor* from 75 million years ago and *Deinonychus* dating back 110 million years. Raptors varied in size from about 2–5 metres long. All these meat-eaters were in the main dinosaur group called the theropods, or 'bird feet'.

◀ *Compsognathus* chased small prey such as lizards and bugs.

Close cousins

261 In the tyrannosaur group with *T rex* were several of its closest relatives. They were big, fierce dinosaurs, but most lived before *T rex* and were not quite as large.

262 *Albertosaurus* is named after a princess. Its fossils come from the Canadian province Alberta, which was named in honour of Louise Caroline Alberta, daughter of Britain's Queen Victoria and Prince Albert.

▲ There are many fossil remains of *Gorgosaurus*, making it one of the best known of all the tyrannosaurs. It had a small horn-like crest above each eye.

263 Fossils of *Gorgosaurus*, 'fierce lizard', come mainly from Alberta, Canada and are 75–70 million years old. *Gorgosaurus* was very similar to *Albertosaurus*, although slightly smaller at 8–9 metres long. Like all tyrannosaurs, it had hollow bones and openings in its skull that helped to reduce its weight. Some experts think that *Gorgosaurus* was really a kind of *Albertosaurus* and that its name should be changed.

264 *Daspletosaurus*, 'frightful lizard', was another dinosaur from Alberta, 80–75 million years ago. Its fossils are also known from other regions of North America, as far south as New Mexico, USA. It was about 8 metres long with especially large jaws and teeth. Its arms were small, but not quite so tiny compared to its body as those of *Tyrannosaurus rex*.

▲ *Daspletosaurus* weighed about 2.5 tonnes and had a skull more than one metre long.

▼ *Alectrosaurus* from Mongolia, Asia was one of the smaller tyrannosaurs, at 5 metres in length.

▶ *Appalachiosaurus* fossils come from Alabama, USA, which is an area where few other tyrannosaurs have been found. Only one 7-metre-long skeleton has been found, but it was probably not fully grown.

265 *Albertosaurus*, 'Alberta lizard', dates from about 75–70 million years ago. Its fossils were first found in Alberta, Canada. It looked similar to *T rex*, with a huge mouth and sharp teeth, small arms and powerful legs, but it was smaller, at 9–10 metres and around 1.5 tonnes. At one site the remains of over 20 *Albertosaurus* were found, from adults to teenagers to youngsters. This could have been a mixed pack out hunting.

Discovering T rex

266 The first fossils of *T rex* were found in the 1870s by Arthur Lakes and John Bell Hatcher, in Wyoming, USA. However these were not recognized as T rex until years later. In 1892, fossil expert Edward Drinker Cope found remains of a big meat-eater and named them *Manospondylus*. Over 100 years later these remains were restudied and renamed as *T rex*.

▲ Edward Drinker Cope (1840–97) named many other kinds of dinosaurs in addition to *T rex*, including *Camarasaurus, Amphicoelias, Coelophysis, Hadrosaurus* and *Monoclonius.*

▶ The fossil bones of big dinosaurs such as *T rex* are solid stone and very heavy. Many years ago, horses dragged them from rocky, remote areas to the nearest road or railway.

267 In 1900, again in Wyoming, leading fossil collector Barnum Brown found the first partial skeleton of *Tyrannosaurus rex*, rather than scattered single bones and teeth. At first the fossils were named as *Dynamosaurus* by Henry Fairfield Osborn of the American Museum of Natural History in New York.

I DON'T BELIEVE IT!

Osborn's report of 1905 included several kinds of dinosaurs. Due to a mix-up with the names, T rex was almost called *Dynamosaurus imperiosus*. So T rex could have been *D imp!*

268 *T rex* fossils have always been greatly prized by museums, exhibitions and private collectors. In 1941, the fossils that Brown found in 1902 were sold to the Carnegie Museum of Natural History in Pittsburgh, Pennsylvania, for a huge sum of money. Searching for, selling and buying *T rex* fossils continues today.

▼ Barnum Brown was the most famous fossil-hunter of his time. He sometimes wore a thick fur coat — even when digging for fossils in the scorching sun.

269 Barnum Brown discovered parts of another *Tyrannosaurus rex* fossil skeleton at Hell Creek, Montana, in 1902. In 1905, Osborn wrote a scientific description of these remains and called them *Tyrannosaurus rex*. This was the first time the official name was used. In a way, it was when *T rex* was 'born'.

BARNUM BROWN — DINOSAUR DETECTIVE

Barnum Brown (1873-1963) collected not only dinosaur fossils, but fossils of all kinds, and other scientific treasures such as crystals. He and his teams worked for the American Museum of Natural History in New York. They travelled to remote places, and if there were rivers but no roads, they used a large raft as a floating base camp. They worked fast too, often blasting apart rocks with dynamite. Brown also made a living by informing oil companies about the best places to drill for oil.

270 In 1906, Brown found an even better part-skeleton of *Tyrannosaurus rex* in Montana. The same year, Osborn realized that the *Dynamosaurus* fossils were extremely similar to *Tyrannosaurus rex*, so he renamed those too as *Tyrannosaurus rex*. The public began to hear about this huge, fierce, meat-eating monster from long ago, and soon its fame was growing fast.

Rebuilding T rex

271 Fossil experts use preserved bones and other parts of *T rex* to show what it looked like when alive. The bones are also compared to those of similar animals alive today, known as comparative anatomy. For *T rex*, similar living animals include crocodiles, lizards – and birds.

272 Some fossil bones have patches, grooves and ridges called 'muscle scars'. They show where the animal's muscles were joined to the bones in life. This helps experts to work out how the muscles pulled the bones and how *T rex* moved when it was alive.

273 As with other extinct creatures, there are no remains of *T rex*'s soft body parts such as the stomach, guts, heart and lungs. These were eaten by scavengers soon after death or were rotted away. However experts can use comparative anatomy with living creatures to imagine what *T rex*'s soft body parts looked like.

▼ Fossil dinosaur skin has a scaly surface, similar to many of today's reptiles.

274 Skin and scales of dinosaurs sometimes form fossils. However they are the colour of the rocks that make the fossils, not the colour of the original skin and scales. So we have no way of knowing *T rex*'s true colour in life.

◄ Close cousins of *T rex* have been preserved with simple hair-like feathers on their skin. It may be possible that *T rex* also had feathers.

▲ This reconstruction of *T rex* shows the modern idea of its body position, with tail held straight out behind. When the skull is moved from the trolley to the front end of the neck bones, it will be positioned low, not high as previously thought.

▶ For many years, *T rex* was thought to hold its head up high and drag its tail along the ground.

275 The first reconstructions of *T rex* showed it standing almost upright like a kangaroo. However from its bone and joint shapes, most experts now think that it held its head and body level with the ground, balanced over its big back legs by its long, heavy tail.

The story of Sue

276 The biggest *Tyrannosaurus rex* found so far is 'Sue'. Its official code number is FMNH PR2081, from the Field Museum of Natural History in Chicago, USA.

277 'Sue' is named after its discoverer, Sue Hendrickson. She was working at a fossil dig in 1990 near the town of Faith, in South Dakota, USA, when she uncovered parts of a massive *T rex*. An entire team of people helped to dig up and clean the remains.

278 With about four-fifths of its teeth, bones and other parts preserved, 'Sue' is amazingly complete for a fossil animal. The dinosaur was probably covered with mud soon after it died, which prevented scavenging animals from cracking open or carrying away its bones.

279 'Sue' dates from between 67 and 65.5 million years ago. It measures 12.8 metres from nose to tail-tip and 4 metres tall at the hips. The weight of 'Sue' when alive was probably between 5.5 and 6.5 tonnes.

◄ Sue Hendrickson with the fossil foot of 'Sue'. As well as finding 'Sue' the *T rex*, Sue Hendrickson is an expert diver and has explored shipwrecks and sunken cities.

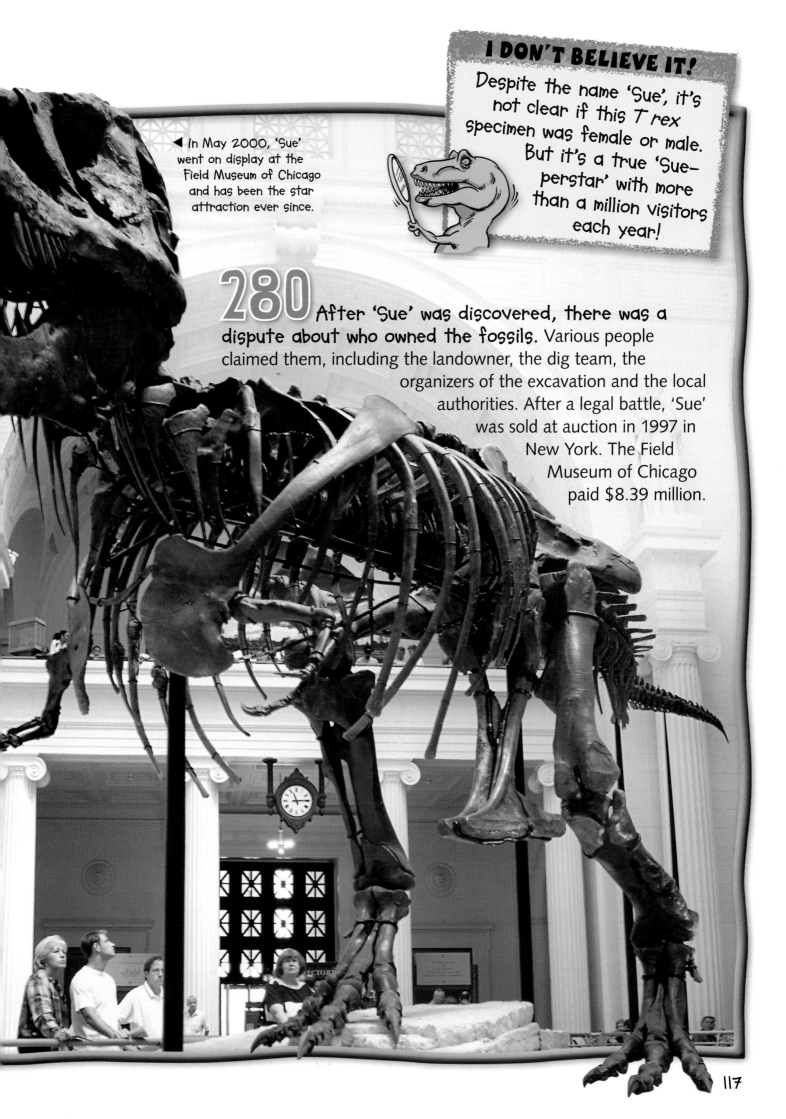

◀ In May 2000, 'Sue' went on display at the Field Museum of Chicago and has been the star attraction ever since.

280 After 'Sue' was discovered, there was a dispute about who owned the fossils. Various people claimed them, including the landowner, the dig team, the organizers of the excavation and the local authorities. After a legal battle, 'Sue' was sold at auction in 1997 in New York. The Field Museum of Chicago paid $8.39 million.

Stan, Jane, and the rest

281 Apart from 'Sue', there are more than 30 other sets of *T rex* fossils. Some are just a few bones and teeth, while others are well preserved, fairly complete skeletons.

282 'Stan' is named after its discoverer Stan Sacrisen. Code numbered BHI 3033, it was dug up near Buffalo, South Dakota, USA in 1992 by a team from the Black Hills Institute. 'Stan' was about 12.2 metres long and 3 tonnes in weight, with 199 bones and 58 teeth. Some bones show signs of injuries that had healed, including broken ribs, a damaged neck and a tooth wound in the skull.

▶ 'Stan' is now at the Black Hills Museum in Hill City, South Dakota.

283 'Wankel rex', specimen MOR 555, was found by Kathy Wankel in 1988. It was excavated by a team from the Museum of the Rockies and is now on show at that museum in Bozeman, Montana.

284 'Tinker', also called 'Kid Rex', was a young *Tyrannosaurus rex*. About two-thirds adult size, it was found in 1998 in South Dakota and named after the leader of the fossil-hunting team, Ron 'Tinker' Frithiof.

285 'Jane' is specimen BMRP 2002.4.1 at the Burpee Museum of Natural History, Rockford, Illinois, USA. Found in Montana, it's smaller than a full grown *Tyrannosaurus rex*, at 6.5 metres long and 650–700 kilograms. Some experts believe it is a part-grown youngster, probably 10–12 years old when it died. Others say it is a similar but smaller kind of dinosaur named *Nanotyrannus*.

▶ The fossils of 'Jane' from Montana's Hell Creek took more than four years to dig out, clean up and put together for display.

NEW NAME FOR *T REX*

You will need:
pictures of *T rex* in different poses
pen   paper

Copy some pictures of *T rex* onto your paper. Imagine you and your friends have discovered their fossils and given them nicknames. Write these next to your drawings. Perhaps *T rex* should be named after you?

286 Until the 1990s, *Tyrannosaurus rex* was famous as the biggest predatory land creature of all time. However the past few years have seen discoveries of even bigger meat-eating dinosaurs.

287 Fossils of *Giganotosaurus*, 'southern giant reptile', were uncovered in 1993 in Patagonia, Argentina. This huge hunter was slightly bigger than *T rex*, at more than 13 metres long and weighing over 6 tonnes. *Giganotosaurus* lived earlier than *T rex*, about 95–90 million years ago.

288 Fossils of *Spinosaurus* were first found in Egypt in 1912. This predator lived 100–95 million years ago, and had long, bony rods sticking up from its back that may have held up a 'sail' of skin. The original remains suggested a big predator, but not as big as *T rex*. However recent finds indicate that *Spinosaurus* may have been larger, maybe 16 metres long and 7 tonnes in weight.

QUIZ

Put these dinosaurs in order of size, biggest to smallest:

rannosaurus rex Deinonychus
Brachiosaurus Spinosaurus
ompsognathus Giganotosaurus

Answers:
Brachiosaurus, Spinosaurus, Giganotosaurus, Tyrannosaurus rex, Deinonychus, Compsognathus

289 *Carcharodontosaurus*, 'shark tooth lizard', was another massive hunter from North Africa. It was first named in 1931 and lived 100–95 million years ago. Recent discoveries in Morocco and Niger show that it could have been about the same size as *T rex*.

290 Another *T rex*-sized dinosaur was *Mapusaurus*, which lived in Argentina around the same time as *T rex* lived in North America. It was not as heavily built as *T rex*, weighing about 3 tonnes.

▼ This skull of *Carcharodontosaurus* measures more than 1.7 metres in length, with teeth 20 centimetres long. The human skull just in front of it gives an idea of just how big this dinosaur was.

▶ *T rex* and the other meat-eaters were not the biggest dinosaurs by far. Much larger are huge plant-eaters such as *Brachiosaurus* and *Argentinosaurus*.

Trex superstar

291 *Tyrannosaurus rex* is far more than a big meat-eating dinosaur. It's a world superstar, alongside such famous creatures as the great white shark, blue whale, gorilla, tiger and golden eagle. If *Tyrannosaurus rex* was alive today and could charge money for using its name, pictures, sponsorships and advertising, it would be mega-rich!

292 *T rex* was one of the stars of the *Jurassic Park* movies. However it didn't live in the Jurassic Period, it lived 80 million years later at the end of the Cretaceous Period.

293 Ever since its fossils were discovered, *T rex* has starred in books, plays and movies. It's featured in films such as *The Lost World* (first made in 1925, then again in 1960 and 1992), several *King Kong* movies, the animated *The Land Before Time* (1988), and the *Night at the Museum* movies (2006, 2009).

▼ In *Night at the Museum*, Rexy the *T rex* skeleton looks fierce but is really quite cute and chases bones like a puppy.

▶ In *T rex: Back to the Cretaceous* (1998), Ally finds a mysterious egg-like rock – which transports her back to the end of the Dinosaur Age.

294
In movies, *Tyrannosaurus rex* is perhaps most famous from the *Jurassic Park* series. These began with *Jurassic Park* itself in 1993, then *The Lost World: Jurassic Park* in 1997, and *Jurassic Park 3* in 2001. *Tyrannosaurus rex* is shown breaking out of its fenced enclosure, attacking people and generally causing havoc – but also looking after and protecting its baby with great care.

295
Toy Story movies, games and other products feature an unusual *Tyrannosaurus rex* toy called 'Rex' who is nervous, weedy and worried. This is very unlike the usual fearsome character given to *T rex*.

▶ The *T rex* of *Jurassic Park* tries to sniff out human prey, but in the end it saves them from being attacked by marauding raptor dinosaurs.

What next for *Trex*?

296 Why did *T rex* die out 66 million years ago, along with all other dinosaurs? The main suggestion is that a huge lump of rock from space, an asteroid, hit Earth and caused worldwide disasters of giant waves, volcanic eruptions and a dust cloud that blotted out the Sun. In this end-of Cretaceous mass extinction no dinosaurs, not even the great *T rex*, could survive.

▶ A dinosaur fan comes face to face with *T rex* at the *Walking with Dinosaurs* tour, 2009. Animatronic (mechanical model) dinosaurs move and roar, but unlike the real ones, they are harmless.

297 Our ideas about *T rex* do not stand still. As scientists discover more fossils and invent new methods of studying them, we learn more about *T rex* and the other animals and plants of its time.

298 Could *Tyrannosaurus rex* or similar dinosaurs still survive today, in thick jungle or on remote mountains? Most of the world's land has now been explored or photographed from aircraft and satellites. Sadly, there's no sign of *T rex* or other big unknown animals.

299 Could *T rex* somehow be brought back to life from its fossil remains? Even with the latest scientific methods, this is still a very remote and faraway possibility. Even if it worked, where would *Tyrannosaurus rex* live and what would it eat? Its habitat, with the climate, scenery, plants and animals, is long gone.

300 *Tyrannosaurus rex* no longer holds the record as the biggest land predator of all time. But it's such a well known celebrity around the world that it will probably remain the most famous dinosaur, and one of the most popular creatures of all, for many years to come.

Index

Entries in **bold** refer to main subject entries. Entries in *italics* refer to illustrations

ACKNOWLEDGEMENTS

The publishers would like to thank the following sources for the use of their photographs:
Key: t = top, b = bottom, l = left, r = right, c = centre, bg = background

Alamy 69 (t) petpics; 86 Photos 12
Burpee Museum of Natural History 119
Corbis 52(t) Louie Psihoyos; 56 Layne Kennedy; 58(cl) Louie Psihoyos; 59 Sciepro/Science Photo Library; 69(b) Walter Myers; 73(t) Handout/Reuters; 80(b) Louie Psihoyos; 81(cr) Louie Psihoyos; 96(b); 112 Bettman; 113 Bettman; 114 DK Limited; 118 Louie Psihoyos; 120 Louie Psihoyos
Getty Images 123(t) Handout
Glow Images 35(b) O. Louis Mazzatenta; 82(tl) Lynn Johnson/National Geographic Image Collection, 82(tr) Lynn Johnson/National Geographic Image Collection; 83(l) Lynn Johnson/National Geographic Image Collection
Photolibrary 96(t) Robert Clark; 106 Salvatore Vasapolli; 117 Steve Vider

Reuters 116 Ho Old
Rex Features 122 © 20thC.Fox/Everett; 124 Nils Jorgensen
Science Photo Library 46–47 Jose Antonio Penas; 58–59 Julius T Csotony; 61 Jose Antonio Penas; 66–67 Christian Jegou Publiphoto Diffusion; 73(b) Christian Darkin; 76–77 Steve Munsinger; 78–79 Christian Jegou; 84(t) Natural History Museum, London; 115 Volker Steger
Shutterstock.com front cover Ralf Juergen Kraft; back cover Michael Rosskothen (*Dimorphodon*), kikujungboy (*T rex* skeleton), Andreas Meyer (*Elasmosaurus*); 1 Michael Rosskothen (*Deinonychus*, *Giganotosaurus*, *Pterodactylus*), Catmando (*Brachiosaurus* herd), Eric Broder Van Dyke (dinosaur tracks), Redchanka (fossil); 48–49 Eric Broder Van Dyke; 49(t) Catmando; 50(b) leonello calvetti; 52–53 George Burba; 57(b) Catmando; 60 Michael Rosskothen; 61 Marilyn Volan; 62(t) Kostyantyn Ivanyshen, (c) Linda Bucklin; 63(bl) DM7, (br) Jean-Michel Girard; 70 leonello calvetti; 71(c) Ozja, (b) Ralf Juergen Kraft; 85 SmudgeChris
Topfoto 123(b) Topham Picture Point

All other photographs are from:
DigitalSTOCK, digitalvision, John Foxx, PhotoAlto, PhotoDisc, PhotoEssentials, PhotoPro, Stockbyte

Every effort has been made to acknowledge the source and copyright holder of each picture. Miles Kelly Publishing apologizes for any unintentional errors or omissions.